The Lone Wolf: Harnessing the Power of Solitude for Success

Table of Contents

Chapter one: Introduction: Understanding the Lone Wolf Mindset

What is a Lone Wolf Mindset and Why is it Important to Understand

A lone wolf mindset is a mentality that values independence and self-sufficiency. It is characterized by a strong sense of self, a desire to chart one's own course in life, and a willingness to go against the norm. The lone wolf is not afraid to stand alone, and is often seen as a symbol of strength and resilience.

The origins of the lone wolf mindset can be traced back to ancient Japanese culture. In the samurai culture of feudal Japan, the lone wolf was seen as a revered and respected figure. The samurai were warriors who lived by a code of honor and were expected to be self-reliant and able to act independently. They were also expected to be able to defend themselves against multiple opponents and to be able to survive in harsh conditions. This mindset of self-sufficiency and independence was passed down through generations and is still present in Japanese culture today.

One of the most famous Japanese authors who wrote about the lone wolf mindset is Miyamoto Musashi. He was a renowned swordsman and author of "The Book of Five Rings," a classic text on strategy and martial arts. In his book, Musashi wrote, "The mind of the lone wolf is like the wind, free and unchained. It is not bound by the opinions of others and is not swayed by the opinions of the masses." This quote illustrates the idea that the lone wolf is not constrained by the opinions of others and is free to make their own decisions.

Another famous Japanese author who wrote about the lone wolf mindset is Yojimbo. In his book, "The Lone Wolf," he wrote, "The lone wolf is a symbol of strength and resilience. He is not afraid to stand alone, and is always ready to defend himself against any challenge. He is a true warrior, who lives by his own code of honor and is not afraid to die for it." This quote emphasizes the idea that the lone wolf is a symbol of strength and resilience, and is willing to stand alone and defend their beliefs.

In modern times, the lone wolf mindset is still highly valued in Japanese culture. Many Japanese people still believe in the importance of being self-reliant and independent. They also believe in the importance of being able to make one's own decisions and chart their own course in life.

One modern Japanese author who writes about the lone wolf mindset is Haruki Murakami. In his book, "Kafka on the Shore," he wrote, "The lone wolf is a symbol of freedom and individuality. He is not afraid to be different and to chart his own path in life." This quote illustrates the idea that the lone wolf is a symbol of freedom and individuality, and is not afraid to be different and chart their own course in life.

In addition to being valued in Japanese culture, the lone wolf mindset is also important to understand in the modern world. In today's fast-paced and ever-changing society, the ability to be self-reliant and independent is more important than ever. It is essential to be able to make one's own decisions and chart one's own course in life in order to be successful. The lone wolf mindset also teaches us to be resilient and to not be afraid to stand alone and defend our beliefs.

One modern author who writes about the importance of the lone wolf mindset is Jordan Peterson. In his book, "12 Rules for Life," he wrote, "The lone wolf mindset is important because it teaches us to be self-reliant and independent. It also teaches us to be resilient and to not be afraid to stand alone and defend our beliefs." This quote emphasizes the importance of the lone wolf mindset in teaching us to be self-reliant, independent, and resilient.

In conclusion, the lone wolf mindset is a mentality that values independence and self-sufficiency. It is rooted in ancient Japanese culture, where the samurai were expected to be self-reliant and able to act independently. Famous Japanese authors such as Miyamoto Musashi and Yojimbo have written about the lone wolf mindset and its importance. In modern times, the lone wolf mindset is still highly valued in Japanese culture and is also important to understand in the modern world. It teaches us to be self-reliant, independent, and resilient, and to not be afraid to stand alone and defend our beliefs. The lone wolf mindset is a symbol of freedom, strength, and resilience, and is essential for navigating the ever-changing landscape of the modern world.

The Origins of the Lone Wolf Mindset: A Historical Perspective

The origins of the lone wolf mindset can be traced back to ancient Japan, where the concept of the solitary warrior was celebrated and revered. The lone wolf mindset is characterized by a strong sense of self-reliance, independence, and a desire to forge one's own path in life. This mindset is deeply rooted in Japanese culture and has been passed down through generations, becoming an integral part of Japanese identity.

One of the earliest examples of the lone wolf mindset can be found in the writings of the ancient Japanese poet, Bashō. In his famous haiku, "Over the wintry / Forest, winds howl in rage / With no leaves to blow", Bashō expresses the solitary nature of the lone wolf. The winds howling through the barren forest symbolize the lone wolf's isolation and independence, while the rage of the winds represents the fierce determination and strength of the lone wolf.

Another ancient Japanese author, Musashi Miyamoto, is known for his famous book, "The Book of Five Rings". In this book, Musashi emphasizes the importance of self-reliance and independence in becoming a true warrior. He writes, "The way of the warrior is in desperateness. Ten men or more cannot kill such a man. Common sense will not accomplish great things. Simply become insane and desperate." This quote highlights the lone wolf's willingness to go against the norm and take risks in order to achieve greatness.

The lone wolf mindset is also deeply ingrained in the Japanese samurai culture. The samurai were known for their fierce loyalty and devotion to their lord, but they were also expected to be self-reliant and independent. The famous samurai, Takeda Shingen, once said, "The true meaning of a warrior is to have courage, to be true to oneself, and to be willing to die for what one believes in." This quote encapsulates the essence of the lone wolf mindset, with the emphasis on courage, self-reliance, and the willingness to die for one's beliefs.

The lone wolf mindset has also been celebrated in Japanese literature and film. In the famous Japanese novel, "Lone Wolf and Cub", the main character, Ogami Itto, is a lone wolf who has been betrayed by his clan and must fend for himself and his young son. The novel explores the themes of revenge, loyalty, and the strength of the lone wolf's spirit. Similarly, in the popular Japanese film, "The Last Samurai", the main character, Nathan Algren, is a lone wolf who is initially an outsider but ultimately becomes a samurai and learns the true meaning of honor and courage.

In modern Japan, the lone wolf mindset is still celebrated and revered. The famous Japanese author, Haruki Murakami, has written several novels that explore the theme of the lone wolf. In his novel, "Norwegian Wood", Murakami writes, "I was always alone, even when I was with someone. I was always searching for something, something that I couldn't find." This quote highlights the solitary nature of the lone wolf and their constant search for meaning and purpose in life.

In conclusion, the lone wolf mindset has a rich history in Japan, dating back to ancient times. The concept of the solitary warrior has been celebrated and revered in Japanese culture, literature, and film. Through the writings of Bashō, Musashi Miyamoto, Takeda Shingen, and Haruki Murakami, the lone wolf's self-reliance, independence, and fierce determination have been immortalized. The lone wolf mindset continues to be an integral part of Japanese identity, inspiring generations to forge their own path in life and be true to themselves.

The Impact of Modern Society on the Lone Wolf Mindset

The lone wolf mindset, characterized by independence, self-reliance, and a strong sense of individuality, has been revered in many cultures throughout history. In ancient Japan, for example, the samurai warrior was seen as the epitome of the lone wolf, with their strict code of honor and unwavering commitment to duty. Similarly, in ancient China, the Taoist hermit was seen as a solitary figure who had transcended the material world and achieved enlightenment.

However, in modern society, the lone wolf mindset is often viewed with suspicion and even hostility. The emphasis on conformity and the need to fit in is seen as incompatible with the lone wolf mindset, and those who embrace it are often seen as outsiders or misfits. This has led to a growing sense of isolation and alienation among those who identify as lone wolves, and has raised important questions about the impact of modern society on this mindset.

One of the key ways in which modern society has impacted the lone wolf mindset is through the emphasis on conformity. In today's world, it is often seen as essential to fit in and conform to societal norms in order to be successful. This can be seen in the way that people are expected to conform to certain dress codes, hairstyles, and even attitudes and beliefs in order to be considered "normal."

This emphasis on conformity can be seen as a direct threat to the lone wolf mindset, which values independence and self-reliance above all else. As the famous Japanese author Haruki Murakami writes in his novel "Hard-Boiled Wonderland and the End of the World," "The world is a dangerous place, and people are not trustworthy. That's why you have to rely on yourself."

Similarly, in ancient China, the Taoist philosopher Lao Tzu wrote in the "Tao Te Ching," "The best leader is one the people hardly know exists, one who walks his path in peace." This passage highlights the idea that true strength and wisdom come from embracing one's individuality and following one's own path, rather than conforming to societal norms.

Another way in which modern society has impacted the lone wolf mindset is through the emphasis on materialism. In today's world, there is a constant pressure to acquire more and more possessions, to keep up with the latest trends and fashions, and to present a certain image to the world.

This emphasis on materialism can be seen as another direct threat to the lone wolf mindset, which values simplicity and self-sufficiency above all else. As the Japanese author Yukio Mishima writes in his novel "The Temple of the Golden Pavilion," "The true warrior is the one who is able to live in a world of simplicity, without the need for material possessions."

Similarly, in ancient China, the Taoist philosopher Chuang Tzu wrote in the "Chuang Tzu," "The man who is contented with what he has, will never be poor. The man who is dissatisfied with what he has, will never be rich." This passage highlights the idea that true happiness and fulfillment come from embracing one's individuality and living a simple, unencumbered life, rather than constantly seeking more and more possessions.

The impact of modern society on the lone wolf mindset can also be seen in the way that people are expected to conform to certain social norms and expectations. In today's world, there is a constant pressure to conform to societal norms and expectations, whether it be in terms of gender roles, sexual orientation, or even political beliefs.

This pressure to conform can be seen as another direct threat to the lone wolf mindset, which values independence and self-reliance above all else. As the famous Chinese author Lu Xun writes in his novel "Diary

Challenging the Lone Wolf Mindset: Moving Toward a More Connected Society

The concept of the lone wolf has long been romanticized in society, with the image of a strong, independent individual striking out on their own and conquering their goals without any help from others. However, this mindset has been proven to be harmful, not only to the individual but also to society as a whole. The idea of the lone wolf is a myth that needs to be challenged and replaced with a more connected and cooperative mindset.

The Red Indian Tribe and the Concept of Community

The Red Indian tribe, also known as the Native Americans, is a group of indigenous people who have lived in North America for thousands of years. They have a deep understanding of the importance of community and connection, and their way of life serves as a powerful example of how a more connected society can benefit everyone.

One of the most important aspects of the Red Indian tribe's way of life is their emphasis on community. They believe that the well-being of the individual is closely tied to the well-being of the community as a whole. This is reflected in their use of the term "we" instead of "I" when referring to themselves. For example, a Red Indian might say "We are the Red Indian tribe" instead of "I am a member of the Red Indian tribe."

This emphasis on community is also reflected in their way of life. The Red Indian tribe is known for its strong sense of cooperation and mutual aid. They believe that everyone has something to contribute, and that everyone has the right to receive help when they need it. This is reflected in their practice of sharing resources, such as food and shelter, among the community.

The Red Indian tribe also places a strong emphasis on the importance of connection to the natural world. They believe that humans are not separate from nature, but are a part of it. This is reflected in their practice of living in harmony with the natural world, and their belief in the interconnectedness of all living things.

The Lone Wolf Mindset and its Harmful Effects

The lone wolf mindset is a harmful myth that needs to be challenged. It is based on the idea that the individual is the most important unit in society, and that the individual's success is the most important goal. This mindset is reflected in the way society is organized, with individuals competing against each other for resources and opportunities.

The lone wolf mindset is harmful because it promotes a culture of competition and individualism, which can lead to feelings of isolation and loneliness. It also promotes a culture of consumerism, where people are encouraged to buy things they don't need and to prioritize their own wants and needs above those of others.

The lone wolf mindset also has negative effects on society as a whole. It encourages people to focus on their own individual success, rather than working together to create a better society for everyone. This can lead to a lack of cooperation and a lack of progress in areas such as healthcare, education, and the environment.

Moving Toward a More Connected Society

To move toward a more connected society, we need to challenge the lone wolf mindset and embrace the values of community and cooperation. We need to recognize that the well-being of the individual is closely tied to the well-being of the community as a whole, and that we are all interconnected.

One way to move toward a more connected society is to promote a culture of mutual aid and cooperation. This can be done by encouraging people to share resources, such as food and shelter, among the community. It can also be done by promoting the idea of "we" instead of "I," and by encouraging people to work together to create a better society for everyone.

Another way to move toward a more connected society is toencourage people to connect with nature and recognize their place within it. This can be done by promoting environmental conservation, encouraging sustainable living, and encouraging people to spend more time outdoors.

Practical Examples

There are many practical examples of how we can move toward a more connected society. Some of these include:

1. Community gardens: Encouraging people to come together and grow their own food can promote cooperation, mutual aid, and connection to nature.
2. Time banking: A time banking system allows people to exchange services with each other, without the use of money. This promotes cooperation and mutual aid among the community.
3. Voluntary simplicity: Voluntary simplicity is the practice of living a simple and minimalist lifestyle, with a focus on the things that truly matter. This can help people to disconnect from consumerism and focus on connection with others and nature.
4. Support groups: Support groups can provide a safe and supportive space for people to come together and connect with others who are going through similar experiences. This can help to reduce feelings of isolation and loneliness.
5. Mentorship programs: Mentorship programs can help to connect people of different generations, and can provide a sense of community and belonging.

Conclusion

In conclusion, the lone wolf mindset is a harmful myth that needs to be challenged. The Red Indian tribe serves as a powerful example of how a more connected society can benefit everyone. By promoting a culture of mutual aid and cooperation, connecting with nature, and encouraging community-building initiatives, we can move toward a more connected society where everyone's well-being is prioritized.

"The Red Indian tribe is known for its strong sense of cooperation and mutual aid. They believe that everyone has something to contribute, and that everyone has the right to receive help when they need it."

"The lone wolf mindset is harmful because it promotes a culture of competition and individualism, which can lead to feelings of isolation and loneliness."

"We need to recognize that the well-being of the individual is closely tied to the well-being of the community as a whole, and that we are all interconnected."

"Encouraging people to come together and grow their own food can promote cooperation, mutual aid, and connection to nature."

"Support groups can provide a safe and supportive space for people to come together and connect with others who are going through similar experiences."

"Mentorship programs can help to connect people of different generations, and can provide a sense of community and belonging."

Chapter Two: The Benefits of Solitude: Discovering the Power of Being Alone

Connecting with Yourself: The Importance of Solitude in Self-Discovery

The human experience is a complex and ever-changing one. We are constantly bombarded with external stimuli and are expected to navigate through the chaos of everyday life. It can be easy to lose ourselves in the hustle and bustle of it all, but it is important to remember that true self-discovery and inner peace can only be found through connecting with ourselves. One of the most effective ways to do this is through the practice of solitude.

Solitude is defined as the state of being alone or isolated. It can be a daunting prospect for many people, but it is an essential aspect of self-discovery. In solitude, we are forced to confront our thoughts and emotions, and to truly listen to what our inner selves have to say.

Buddhism, a religion and philosophy that originated in ancient India, places a strong emphasis on the importance of solitude in achieving inner peace and enlightenment. The Buddha himself spent many years in solitude, meditating and contemplating the nature of existence. He believed that by understanding the workings of our own minds, we can break free from the cycle of suffering and attain enlightenment.

One of the key teachings of Buddhism is that true happiness can only be found within ourselves, and not through external means. This is why solitude is so important; it allows us to connect with ourselves and to understand our own minds. The Buddha once said, "In the sky, there is no distinction of east and west; people create distinctions out of their own minds and then believe them to be true." In solitude, we can break free from the distinctions and illusions that we have created in our own minds, and come to a deeper understanding of ourselves and the world around us.

Shaolin monks, who are known for their discipline and mastery of martial arts, also place a strong emphasis on the importance of solitude in their practice. Shaolin monks spend many hours each day in meditation and training, and often live in isolation for extended periods of time. This is not only to improve their physical abilities, but also to deepen their spiritual understanding and connection to themselves.

One Shaolin monk once said, "Solitude is not loneliness, it is a necessary aspect of self-discovery. In solitude, we can learn to listen to the whispers of our own hearts, and find the answers that we seek." Solitude allows us to focus our minds and to tap into our own inner wisdom. It is a time for reflection and contemplation, and can be a powerful tool for self-discovery.

In addition to the spiritual benefits, solitude also has many practical benefits. It allows us to disconnect from the constant distractions of the world, and to focus on our own goals and aspirations. It can also help to reduce stress and anxiety, and improve our overall well-being.

However, it is important to note that solitude does not have to mean complete isolation. It can be found in small moments throughout the day, such as taking a walk in nature, or spending time in silence. The key is to find a balance between connecting with ourselves and the world around us.

In conclusion, solitude is an essential aspect of self-discovery. It allows us to connect with ourselves, understand our own minds, and find inner peace and enlightenment. Buddhism and Shaolin monks both place a strong emphasis on the importance of solitude in their teachings, and it is a powerful tool for anyone looking to deepen their understanding of themselves and the world around them. So, take some time to be alone, and listen to the whispers of your own heart, it will lead you to the answers you seek.

Creativity Unleashed: How Solitude Can Inspire Innovation and Idea Generation

In today's fast-paced world, we are constantly bombarded with distractions and interruptions. We are expected to multitask and be constantly connected, leaving little time for reflection and solitude. However, it is in these quiet and still moments that true creativity and innovation can flourish.

Solitude, or the state of being alone, can provide an individual with the space and freedom to explore new ideas and perspectives. It allows for a deep dive into the self, leading to a greater understanding of one's own thoughts, emotions, and desires. As the famous Buddhist monk and teacher Thich Nhat Hanh states, "Solitude is the ground for the deepest communication. When we are able to be alone, we can enter into the deepest communication with ourselves."

Solitude also allows for a disconnection from external influences and societal pressures. It allows for a break from the constant noise and distractions of the world, providing a clear and focused mind. This clarity of mind can lead to a heightened state of creativity and idea generation. As the Shaolin monk and martial artist Shi Heng Yi states, "In solitude, you can find your true self and unlock your true potential."

One of the most notable examples of how solitude can inspire creativity and innovation is the story of Steve Jobs. Jobs, the co-founder of Apple, was known for his love of solitude and would often retreat to his backyard shed to work on new ideas. In an interview with Walter Isaacson, Jobs stated, "I would go out to the back shed and think about the thing I was working on. I would try to make connections. It's a way to get your mind free of distractions." It was during these moments of solitude that Jobs was able to come up with some of his most groundbreaking ideas, including the development of the Macintosh computer and the iPhone.

Another example of how solitude can inspire creativity and innovation is in the field of science. In the early 20th century, Albert Einstein was working as a patent clerk in Bern, Switzerland. During his free time, Einstein would often take long walks alone, during which he would reflect on the nature of space and time. It was during these solitary moments that Einstein came up with his groundbreaking theory of relativity. As Einstein himself stated, "I often think in music. I live my daydreams in music. I see my life in terms of music."

In the field of art, the famous painter Vincent van Gogh also found inspiration in solitude. Van Gogh often spent long periods of time alone in the countryside, where he would paint some of his most iconic works. In a letter to his brother Theo, van Gogh wrote, "I am seeking, I am striving, I am in it with all my heart." It was during these solitary moments that van Gogh was able to tap into his deepest emotions and create some of his most moving and powerful paintings.

Solitude can also inspire creativity and innovation in the workplace. In today's fast-paced business world, it can be easy to get caught up in the hustle and bustle of daily tasks and meetings. However, taking even a few minutes of solitude can allow for a break from these distractions and provide the space for new ideas to surface. As the Shaolin monk and business consultant Shi Heng Dong states, "Solitude allows for a deeper connection with your inner self and the ability to see things from a different perspective."

In conclusion, solitude can be a powerful tool for inspiration and idea generation. It allows for a disconnection from external distractions and societal pressures, providing a clear and focused mind. It also allows for a deeper understanding of one's own thoughts, emotions, and desires, leading to a heightened state of creativity. Whether in the fields of science, art, business or any other field, solitude can be the key to unlocking new ideas and perspectives.

In order to tap into the power of solitude, it is important to set aside time for quiet reflection and disconnection from the world. This can be done through practices such as meditation, journaling, or simply taking a walk in nature. Additionally, it is important to let go of any societal pressures or expectations to be constantly connected and productive. As the Buddhist monk and teacher Pema Chodron states, "Solitude gives birth to the original in us, to beauty unfamiliar and perilous - to poetry. But also, it gives birth to the opposite: to the perverse, the illicit, the absurd."

In order to unleash our creativity and generate new ideas, we must embrace solitude and allow ourselves the space and freedom to explore new perspectives. As the Shaolin monk and martial artist Shi Heng Yi states, "In solitude, you can find your true self and unlock your true potential." By embracing solitude, we can tap into the boundless creativity and innovation that lies within us.

Escape from Distraction: The Role of Solitude in Focusing the Mind

In today's fast-paced world, it can be difficult to find time to focus on one's thoughts and goals. We are constantly bombarded with distractions, from social media notifications to endless emails and text messages. This constant state of distraction can be detrimental to our mental and emotional well-being, as well as our ability to accomplish our goals.

One way to combat this constant state of distraction is to seek out solitude. Solitude is defined as the state of being alone, without the presence of others. It is a time to disconnect from the distractions of the world and focus on one's thoughts and goals.

Ancient Chinese and Japanese philosophers have long recognized the importance of solitude in achieving a focused mind. Confucius, a Chinese philosopher, once said, "By three methods we may learn wisdom: First, by reflection, which is the noblest; Second, by imitation, which is easiest; and third by experience, which is the bitterest." This quote highlights the importance of reflection, which can only be achieved through solitude.

Another Chinese philosopher, Lao Tzu, also recognized the importance of solitude in achieving a focused mind. He wrote in the Tao Te Ching, "Nature does not hurry, yet everything is accomplished." This quote highlights the importance of taking the time to slow down and focus on one's thoughts and goals, which can only be achieved through solitude.

Japanese philosopher, Basho, also recognized the importance of solitude in achieving a focused mind. He wrote in his book, The Narrow Road to the Deep North, "Do not seek to follow in the footsteps of the men of old; seek what they sought." This quote highlights the importance of finding one's own path, which can only be achieved through solitude.

In today's fast-paced world, it can be difficult to find time to focus on one's thoughts and goals. We are constantly bombarded with distractions, from social media notifications to endless emails and text messages. This constant state of distraction can be detrimental to our mental and emotional well-being, as well as our ability to accomplish our goals.

One way to combat this constant state of distraction is to seek out solitude. Solitude is defined as the state of being alone, without the presence of others. It is a time to disconnect from the distractions of the world and focus on one's thoughts and goals.

For example, imagine you are a college student trying to study for an exam. You are sitting at your desk surrounded by textbooks, notes, and your laptop. However, you find yourself constantly getting distracted by your phone buzzing with notifications, your roommate's TV playing in the background, and the constant chatter of students outside your door. In this scenario, you may find it helpful to seek out solitude in order to focus on your studies. This could mean finding a quiet, secluded spot on campus, or even going to a local library where you can study in peace and quiet.

Another example of how solitude can help us focus our mind is in the professional world. Imagine you are a busy executive who is constantly on the go, attending meetings, conference calls, and networking events. You may find yourself struggling to focus on your work and make important decisions. In this scenario, you may find it helpful to take a break from the constant distractions and seek out solitude. This could mean going for a walk in nature, or even taking a mini-retreat to a remote location where you can clear your mind and focus on your work.

In both of these examples, we can see how solitude can help us focus our mind and achieve our goals. However, it is important to note that solitude is not just about physically being alone, but also about disconnecting from distractions and finding a mental and emotional space to focus. This can be achieved through meditation, journaling, or even just spending time in nature.

One practical way to incorporate solitude into your daily routine is to set aside a specific time each day for quiet reflection. This could be as simple as taking a few minutes to sit in silence and clear your mind, or even taking a short walk in nature. By setting aside this time each day, you are creating a habit of solitude that will help you focus your mind and achieve your goals.

Another way to incorporate solitude into your daily routine is to disconnect from distractions. This could mean turning off your phone or disconnecting from social media for a set period of time each day. By disconnecting from these distractions, you are creating a space for yourself to focus on your thoughts and goals.

It is also important to note that solitude does not have to be a solitary activity. Many people find that practicing yoga or meditation in a group setting can be a beneficial way to achieve a focused mind. Additionally, spending time in nature with friends or family can also provide a sense of solitude and focus.

In conclusion, solitude is an important tool in achieving a focused mind. By disconnecting from distractions and finding a mental and emotional space to focus, we can achieve our goals and improve our mental and emotional well-being. Ancient Chinese and Japanese philosophers have long recognized the importance of solitude in achieving a focused mind, and we can learn from their wisdom to incorporate solitude into our daily lives. As Basho wrote, "Do not seek to follow in the footsteps of the men of old; seek what they sought." It is important to find our own path and seek out solitude in order to focus our mind and achieve our goals.

Finding Inner Peace: How Solitude Can Help You Achieve Mindfulness and Emotional Wellbeing

Inner peace is a state of being that is highly coveted yet often elusive. It is a state of emotional and mental balance that allows us to navigate the challenges of life with equanimity and grace. Finding inner peace is not easy, and it requires a willingness to look within ourselves and to make changes in our lives. One of the most powerful tools for achieving inner peace is solitude. Solitude is the practice of being alone with oneself, and it can be an incredibly transformative experience. In this essay, we will explore how solitude can help us achieve mindfulness and emotional wellbeing. We will also look at some practical life experience examples of how solitude has helped others achieve inner peace.

The Power of Solitude

Solitude is a powerful tool for achieving inner peace because it allows us to step back from the chaos of our lives and to focus on ourselves. When we are alone, we are free from distractions, and we can turn our attention inward. This can be a powerful experience because it allows us to connect with ourselves on a deeper level. We can examine our thoughts and feelings, and we can gain a deeper understanding of who we are.

One of the most powerful benefits of solitude is that it allows us to practice mindfulness. Mindfulness is the practice of being fully present in the moment, and it is a key component of inner peace. When we are alone, we have the opportunity to focus on the present moment, and we can let go of our worries about the future and regrets about the past. This can be a powerful experience because it allows us to let go of our stress and to find peace in the present moment.

"The mind can go in a thousand directions, but on this beautiful path, I walk in peace. With each step, the wind blows. With each step, a butterfly flutters by. Life is a beautiful walk, and I walk in peace." -Thich Nhat Hanh

Solitude can also help us to achieve emotional wellbeing. Emotional wellbeing is the state of being emotionally healthy, and it is an essential component of inner peace. When we are alone, we can take the time to process our emotions, and we can learn to understand and accept them. This can be a powerful experience because it allows us to let go of the emotions that are holding us back and to find peace in our hearts.

"To be alone is to be different, to be different is to be alone." -Suwannaphum

Practical Life Experience Examples

There are many practical life experience examples of how solitude can help us achieve inner peace. Here are a few examples:

1. A woman who had been struggling with anxiety and depression decided to take a solo trip to a remote cabin in the woods. During her time alone, she was able to focus on herself and to process her emotions. She found that by being alone, she was able to let go of her worries and to find peace in the present moment.

2. A man who had been feeling overwhelmed by his job decided to take a week off and to go on a solo camping trip. During his time alone, he was able to let go of his stress and to focus on being present in the moment. He found that by being alone, he was able to find peace in the present moment and to return to work with a renewed sense of purpose.

3. A woman who had been struggling with a difficult relationship decided to take a solo retreat. During her time alone, she was able to process her emotions and to understand her feelings. She found that by being alone, she was able to let go of the emotions that were holding her back and to find peace in her heart.

Conclusion

Inner peace is a state of being that is highly coveted yet often elusive. It is a state of emotional and mental balance that allows us to navigate the challenges of life with equanimity and grace. Finding inner peace is not easy, and it requires a willingness to look within ourselves and to make changes in our lives. One of the most powerful tools for achieving inner peace is solitude. Solitude is the practice of being alone with oneself, and it can be an incredibly transformative experience. In this essay, we explored how solitude can help us achieve mindfulness and emotional wellbeing. We also looked at some practical life experience examples of how solitude has helped others achieve inner peace.

Solitude is a powerful tool for achieving inner peace because it allows us to step back from the chaos of our lives and to focus on ourselves. When we are alone, we are free from distractions, and we can turn our attention inward. This can be a powerful experience because it allows us to connect with ourselves on a deeper level. We can examine our thoughts and feelings, and we can gain a deeper understanding of who we are.

One of the most powerful benefits of solitude is that it allows us to practice mindfulness. Mindfulness is the practice of being fully present in the moment, and it is a key component of inner peace. When we are alone, we have the opportunity to focus on the present moment, and we can let go of our worries about the future and regrets about the past. This can be a powerful experience because it allows us to let go of our stress and to find peace in the present moment.

Solitude can also help us to achieve emotional wellbeing. Emotional wellbeing is the state of being emotionally healthy, and it is an essential component of inner peace. When we are alone, we can take the time to process our emotions, and we can learn to understand and accept them. This can be a powerful experience because it allows us to let go of the emotions that are holding us back and to find peace in our hearts.

In conclusion, solitude is a powerful tool for achieving inner peace. It allows us to step back from the chaos of our lives and to focus on ourselves. It allows us to practice mindfulness and to achieve emotional wellbeing. If you are struggling to find inner peace, consider taking some time for yourself and practicing solitude. You may be surprised by how much it can help you achieve the inner peace that you desire.

"Solitude is not something you must hope for in the future. Rather, it is a deepening of the present, and unless you look for it in the present you will never find it." -Thomas Merton

Chapter Three: Overcoming Social Pressures: Defining Your Own Path

Navigating the Pressure to Conform: Finding Your Own Way

In today's society, there is an overwhelming pressure to conform to societal norms and expectations. From the way we dress, to the way we speak, to the careers we pursue, there is a constant push to fit in and be like everyone else. However, conforming to societal expectations can often lead to a loss of individuality and a sense of emptiness. It is important to recognize the pressure to conform and learn how to navigate it in order to find your own way in life.

One Thai author, Thich Nhat Hanh, writes, "The most precious gift we can offer others is our presence. When mindfulness embraces those we love, they will bloom like flowers." This quote highlights the importance of being present in our own lives and not getting lost in the pressure to conform. By being mindful and present, we can find our own way and not get caught up in the expectations of others.

Another author, Chinese philosopher Confucius, writes, "It does not matter how slow you go as long as you do not stop." This quote emphasizes the importance of perseverance and not giving up on finding your own way, even if it takes longer than expected. The pressure to conform can often make us feel like we are not making progress, but it is important to remember that progress, no matter how small, is still progress.

Russian author Fyodor Dostoevsky writes, "The most stupid of all stupidities is to be afraid of what others will think of you." This quote highlights the importance of not being afraid to be different and not conforming to societal expectations. The pressure to conform can often make us feel like we need to hide our true selves in order to fit in, but it is important to remember that being ourselves is what makes us unique and valuable.

In order to navigate the pressure to conform, it is important to take the time to reflect on our own values and beliefs. We should ask ourselves, what is important to us? What are our passions and goals? By understanding our own values, we can begin to make decisions that align with them, rather than conforming to societal expectations.

Another way to navigate the pressure to conform is to surround ourselves with people who support and encourage our individuality. By having a support system of people who understand and accept us for who we are, we can feel more confident in our own unique path.

Additionally, it is important to remember that failure is not the opposite of success, it is simply a part of the journey. The pressure to conform can often make us feel like we need to be perfect in order to fit in, but it is important to remember that failure is a natural part of the process of finding our own way.

In conclusion, navigating the pressure to conform can be a difficult task, but it is important to remember that our individuality is what makes us unique and valuable. By taking the time to reflect on our own values, surrounding ourselves with people who support and encourage us, and not fearing failure, we can find our own way in life. As Thich Nhat Hanh writes, "When mindfulness embraces those we love, they will bloom like flowers." By embracing our own individuality, we can bloom into the unique and beautiful individuals we were meant to be.

Breaking the Mold: Defying Social Expectations is a powerful concept that encourages individuals to challenge the status quo and forge their own paths in life. It is a call to action for people to look beyond the expectations and stereotypes that society has placed upon them, and to embrace their unique talents and passions.

One of the most powerful examples of breaking the mold comes from the story of Thich Nhat Hanh, a renowned Buddhist monk and peace activist from Vietnam. Thich Nhat Hanh defied the expectations of his family and community by becoming a monk, despite the fact that it was not a traditional path for someone of his background. He went on to become one of the most influential spiritual leaders of our time, spreading the message of peace and compassion throughout the world.

In an interview, Thich Nhat Hanh once said, "The greatest gift you can give someone is your own happiness. If you are truly happy, you can be an instrument of peace, and you can help others to be happy too." This quote illustrates the power of breaking the mold, as Thich Nhat Hanh's decision to pursue a non-traditional path led to him becoming a source of happiness and inspiration for countless others.

Another powerful example of breaking the mold comes from the story of Liu Xiaobo, a Chinese human rights activist and Nobel Peace Prize laureate. Liu Xiaobo defied the expectations of his government by speaking out against corruption and human rights abuses in China. Despite facing harassment and imprisonment for his activism, Liu Xiaobo never wavered in his commitment to speaking out for the rights of the oppressed.

In one of his most famous speeches, Liu Xiaobo said, "Freedom is not something that can be given or taken away. It is something that people must claim for themselves." This quote illustrates the power of breaking the mold, as Liu Xiaobo's decision to speak out against injustice led to him becoming a powerful voice for freedom and human rights in China.

Finally, we turn to the story of Anna Akhmatova, a renowned Russian poet and writer who defied the expectations of Soviet society by continuing to write and publish her work despite the censorship and repression of the Soviet government. Akhmatova's work often dealt with themes of love, loss, and the human condition, and she became one of the most important voices of her generation.

In one of her most famous poems, Akhmatova wrote, "I have lived through much: / as no one on earth has before. / I know how to live, / how to suffer and how to die." This quote illustrates the power of breaking the mold, as Akhmatova's decision to continue writing and publishing her work despite the repression of the Soviet government led to her becoming one of the most important voices of her generation.

In conclusion, breaking the mold and defying social expectations can be a powerful and transformative experience. The stories of Thich Nhat Hanh, Liu Xiaobo, and Anna Akhmatova demonstrate the power of challenging the status quo, and how doing so can lead to a life of purpose, meaning, and impact. As these individuals have shown, breaking the mold is not just about defying expectations, but also about embracing your unique talents and passions, and using them to make a positive impact on the world.

Embracing Your Uniqueness: Defining Your Own Path

In today's society, it's easy to feel pressure to conform to societal norms and expectations. However, true happiness and fulfillment can only be achieved by embracing and celebrating our unique qualities and talents. By defining our own path and staying true to ourselves, we can live a life that is authentic and fulfilling.

One practical example of embracing uniqueness can be seen in the career choices we make. Many of us may feel pressure to pursue a traditional career path, such as becoming a doctor or lawyer, simply because it's what is expected of us. However, if you have a passion for something else, such as art or music, it's important to consider pursuing that instead. As author Brené Brown says, "When we are living in accordance with our values, we are living a wholehearted life." By following our passions and interests, we are living a life that is true to ourselves and brings us joy and fulfillment.

Another practical example of embracing uniqueness can be seen in our relationships. In today's society, there is a certain image of what a "perfect" relationship should look like. However, it's important to remember that every relationship is unique and different. It's important to not compare our relationships to others and instead focus on what works for us and our partner. As author Elizabeth Gilbert says, "The only thing that will make you happy is being happy with who you are, and not who people think you are." By accepting and embracing the unique qualities of our relationships, we can create a deeper connection with our partner and truly be happy.

Embracing uniqueness can also be seen in the way we present ourselves to the world. Society often puts pressure on us to conform to certain beauty standards and expectations. However, it's important to remember that true beauty comes from within and embracing our unique qualities and imperfections. As author Rupi Kaur says, "The world will tell you to hurry, to race against time. But the truth is, there is time enough for everything you want to do, everything you want to be." By embracing our unique beauty, we can confidently present ourselves to the world and radiate confidence and self-love.

In order to truly embrace our uniqueness, it's important to let go of the fear of judgement and comparison. Society often pressures us to compare ourselves to others and strive for perfection. However, as author Brené Brown says, "Perfectionism is not the same thing as striving to be your best. Perfectionism is not about healthy achievement and growth; it's a shield." By letting go of the fear of judgement and comparison, we can focus on embracing our unique qualities and talents and strive to be the best version of ourselves.

It's also important to remember that embracing our uniqueness doesn't mean that we can't learn and grow from others. In fact, by surrounding ourselves with people who have different perspectives and experiences, we can gain a deeper understanding of ourselves and the world around us. As author Maya Angelou says, "I did then what I knew how to do. Now that I know better, I do better." By learning from others, we can continue to grow and evolve as individuals.

In conclusion, embracing our uniqueness is essential for living a fulfilling and authentic life. By defining our own path, staying true to ourselves, and letting go of the fear of judgement and comparison, we can confidently present ourselves to the world and radiate confidence and self-love. Remember, as author Oscar Wilde says, "Be yourself; everyone else is already taken." Embrace your unique qualities and talents, and let them guide you on your own personal journey.

Resisting Peer Pressure: Charting Your Own Course

Peer pressure is a powerful force that can shape our lives and influence our decisions. It is the pressure that we feel from our peers to conform to their beliefs, values, and behaviors. Peer pressure can be positive or negative, but it is often associated with negative consequences such as drug use, alcohol abuse, and risky behaviors. Resisting peer pressure is an essential skill that can help us to chart our own course in life and make decisions that are true to ourselves. In this article, we will explore the nature of peer pressure, the dangers of giving in to peer pressure, and practical strategies for resisting peer pressure with examples from African authors.

The Nature of Peer Pressure

Peer pressure is a normal part of human socialization. It is the influence that our peers have on our beliefs, values, and behaviors. Peer pressure can be positive or negative, and it can come in many forms. For example, positive peer pressure can encourage us to study hard, stay in school, or stay away from drugs and alcohol. Negative peer pressure can encourage us to engage in risky behaviors, such as drug use or drinking, or to conform to negative stereotypes.

Peer pressure is particularly powerful during adolescence, as young people are trying to find their place in the world and are more susceptible to the influence of their peers. During this time, young people are also more likely to engage in risky behaviors, such as drug use and alcohol abuse.

The Dangers of Giving in to Peer Pressure

Giving in to peer pressure can have serious negative consequences, both in the short-term and long-term. For example, engaging in risky behaviors such as drug use or alcohol abuse can lead to serious health problems, such as addiction or overdose. It can also lead to legal problems, such as arrest and incarceration.

Giving in to peer pressure can also have long-term consequences for our mental and emotional well-being. For example, conforming to negative stereotypes or engaging in risky behaviors can lead to feelings of shame, guilt, and low self-esteem. It can also lead to social isolation, as we may feel like we do not fit in with our peers.

African authors have also written about the negative consequences of giving in to peer pressure. Nigerian author Chimamanda Ngozi Adichie writes in her book "Americanah", "To be an individual is to be different, to have a voice that is not the echo of others." Giving in to peer pressure means losing our individuality and conforming to the beliefs and behaviors of others, rather than finding our own voice and charting our own course in life.

South African author Zakes Mda writes in his book "The Madonna of Excelsior", "The pressure to conform to the norm is always present, but true individuals refuse to be swayed by it." Giving in to peer pressure means conforming to the norm and losing our unique perspective and voice in the world.

Practical Strategies for Resisting Peer Pressure

Resisting peer pressure is an essential skill that can help us to chart our own course in life and make decisions that are true to ourselves. Here are some practical strategies for resisting peer pressure:

1. Know Yourself: It is important to understand your own beliefs, values, and goals in life. When we know ourselves, we are better able to resist the influence of our peers and make decisions that are true to ourselves.

2. Build Strong Relationships: Building strong relationships with friends and family who share our values and beliefs can provide a support system that can help us to resist peer pressure.

3. Speak Up: When we speak up and express our own opinions and thoughts, we are less likely to be swayed by the opinions of others. It's important to be assertive and stand up for ourselves, even if it means going against the crowd.

4. Practice Saying No: It's important to practice saying no in a calm and confident manner. This can help us to be more comfortable and assertive when we need to resist peer pressure in real-life situations.

5. Think About the Consequences: Before making a decision, it's important to think about the potential consequences of our actions. This can help us to make more informed and responsible decisions, and to resist peer pressure that may lead us to make poor choices.
6. Find positive role models: Surround yourself with positive role models who make good decisions, this will help you to see the consequences of bad decisions and make better choices for yourself.
7. Be confident and comfortable with yourself: Believe in yourself and your own abilities, and don't be afraid to be different from your peers. Being confident in who you are can make it easier to resist peer pressure and make decisions that align with your values and beliefs.

Chapter Four: Building Self-Reliance: Developing Your Inner Strength

Embracing Failure: Learning from Mistakes

Embracing failure and learning from mistakes is a crucial aspect of personal and professional growth. The fear of failure often holds people back from taking risks and trying new things, but it is through failure that we learn and grow. As the famous author J.K. Rowling said, "It is impossible to live without failing at something, unless you live so cautiously that you might as well not have lived at all."

One real-life example of embracing failure and learning from mistakes is the story of Walt Disney. Disney's first animation studio, Laugh-O-Gram, went bankrupt in 1923, and Disney himself was left with just $40 in his pocket. Instead of giving up on his dream, Disney used this failure as a learning experience and went on to create the Disney Empire we know today. He is quoted as saying, "All our dreams can come true, if we have the courage to pursue them."

Another example is the story of Steve Jobs, co-founder of Apple. After being fired from his own company in 1985, Jobs went on to create the computer animation studio Pixar and eventually returned to Apple, leading the company to even greater success than before. Jobs understood the value of failure and learning from mistakes, saying "I'm convinced that about half of what separates the successful entrepreneurs from the non-successful ones is pure perseverance."

In the business world, embracing failure and learning from mistakes is crucial for innovation and growth. As the CEO of Virgin Group, Richard Branson, states, "Business opportunities are like buses, there's always another one coming." Failure is often seen as a setback, but it can actually open doors to new opportunities. In fact, many successful entrepreneurs have failed multiple times before achieving success.

In personal development, embracing failure and learning from mistakes is important for self-awareness and self-improvement. As author Brené Brown writes, "Owning our story and loving ourselves through that process is the bravest thing that we will ever do." Failing and making mistakes allows us to learn from our actions and make better choices in the future.

One practical strategy for embracing failure and learning from mistakes is to reframe the way we think about failure. Instead of seeing it as a negative event, we can view it as a learning opportunity. As author and motivational speaker Tony Robbins says, "The only real failure is the failure to learn from failure." By changing our mindset and focusing on the lessons we can learn from our mistakes, we can turn failure into a positive experience.

Another strategy is to take responsibility for our actions and not blame others. As author and motivational speaker Zig Ziglar says, "The only way you can fail is if you quit." Taking responsibility for our actions allows us to learn from our mistakes and make improvements for the future.

Embracing failure and learning from mistakes is also about being resilient and not giving up. As author and motivational speaker Norman Vincent Peale says, "Shoot for the moon. Even if you miss, you'll land among the stars." Failure is a part of life, and it's important to not let it defeat us, but instead to use it as motivation to keep going and reach for our goals.

In conclusion, embracing failure and learning from mistakes is essential for personal and professional growth. Failure is not something to be feared, but rather an opportunity to learn and improve. As J.K. Rowling said, "It is impossible to live without failing at something, unless you live so cautiously that you might as well not have lived at all." Embracing failure and learning from our mistakes allows us to become more resilient and achieve success in both our personal and professional lives.

Overcoming Fear: Taking Risks and Stepping Out of Your Comfort Zone

Overcoming fear is a vital part of personal growth and development. Fear can hold us back from achieving our goals, trying new things, and living life to the fullest. However, by taking risks and stepping out of our comfort zones, we can learn to overcome our fears and lead more fulfilling lives.

One of the first steps in overcoming fear is to understand that it is a natural part of the human experience. As author Brené Brown states, "Fear is not something to be conquered, but something to be understood." By recognizing that fear is a normal part of the human experience, we can begin to approach it with curiosity and compassion, rather than judgement and shame.

Another important step in overcoming fear is to acknowledge and accept it. As author and motivational speaker Tony Robbins says, "The only way to overcome fear is to face it head on." By accepting that fear is a part of the process, we can begin to take small steps to face it and work through it.

One way to face fear is by taking small risks. For example, if you're afraid of public speaking, you might start by giving a small presentation to a group of friends or family members. As you become more comfortable with speaking in front of small groups, you can gradually work your way up to larger audiences. By taking small risks, you can begin to build confidence and overcome your fear.

Another way to overcome fear is by stepping out of your comfort zone. As author and motivational speaker Jim Rohn states, "The only way to do great work is to love what you do. If you haven't found it yet, keep looking. Don't settle. As with all matters of the heart, you'll know when you find it." By stepping out of our comfort zones and trying new things, we can discover new passions and talents, and lead more fulfilling lives.

For example, if you're afraid of heights, you might start by taking a small hike or going to the top of a tall building. As you become more comfortable with heights, you can gradually work your way up to more challenging activities such as rock climbing or skydiving. By stepping out of your comfort zone, you can overcome your fear and discover new experiences that you never thought possible.

Another way to overcome fear is by seeking support from others. As author and motivational speaker John C. Maxwell states, “Leadership is not about being in charge. It is about taking care of those in your charge.” By seeking support from friends, family, and professionals, we can begin to work through our fears and overcome them.

For example, if you're afraid of failure, you might seek out the advice and support of a mentor or coach. They can provide guidance and support as you work through your fear and learn to embrace failure as a necessary part of growth and development.

In conclusion, overcoming fear is a vital part of personal growth and development. By understanding that fear is a natural part of the human experience, acknowledging and accepting it, taking small risks, stepping out of our comfort zone, and seeking support from others, we can begin to overcome our fears and lead more fulfilling lives. As author and motivational speaker Eric Thomas says, “When you want to succeed as bad as you want to breathe, then you'll be successful.” Remember to take baby steps, be patient with yourself, and give yourself credit for the progress you make, no matter how small it may be.

Finding Inner Peace: Cultivating Mindfulness and Self-Awareness

Finding inner peace can be a challenging task, especially in a world that is constantly filled with distractions and stressors. However, cultivating mindfulness and self-awareness can be powerful tools in the pursuit of inner peace. Mindfulness is the practice of being present in the moment and paying attention to our thoughts, feelings, and physical sensations. Self-awareness is the ability to understand our own thoughts, feelings, and behaviors, and how they impact our lives. Together, mindfulness and self-awareness can help us to find inner peace and live a more fulfilling life.

One way to cultivate mindfulness and self-awareness is through meditation. Meditation is a practice that involves focusing the mind on a specific object, thought, or activity to achieve a mentally clear and emotionally calm state. As the famous Zen master Thich Nhat Hanh once said, "The practice of mindfulness is the practice of peace." When we are mindful, we are less likely to be swept up in the chaos of our thoughts and emotions, and more able to find inner peace.

Another way to cultivate mindfulness and self-awareness is through journaling. Keeping a journal can help us to track our thoughts, feelings, and behaviors, and to gain insight into our patterns and habits. As the author Julia Cameron writes in her book "The Artist's Way," "Writing is one way of achieving self-discovery. It is the easiest way to learn the most about yourself." By journaling, we can become more self-aware and make conscious choices that align with our values and goals.

Additionally, cultivating mindfulness and self-awareness can also involve actively paying attention to our physical sensations and emotions. This can be done through practices such as yoga, tai chi, or even simply taking a walk in nature. By paying attention to our bodies, we can learn to identify and release tension and stress, which can help us to find inner peace. As the author and meditation teacher Jack Kornfield writes, "The body is our gateway to the present moment, to peace, and to joy."

Furthermore, practicing gratitude and kindness can also be a powerful way to cultivate mindfulness and self-awareness. When we focus on the things we are grateful for and actively try to be kind and compassionate towards others, we can shift our attention away from our own problems and towards the world around us. This can help us to find inner peace and live a more fulfilling life. As the author and speaker Brené Brown writes, "Gratitude and kindness are not only good for our souls, but for our bodies, minds, and relationships as well."

In conclusion, finding inner peace can be a challenging task, but cultivating mindfulness and self-awareness can be powerful tools in the pursuit of inner peace. Whether it's through meditation, journaling, paying attention to our physical sensations and emotions, practicing gratitude and kindness, or any combination of these practices, mindfulness and self-awareness can help us to find inner peace and live a more fulfilling life. As the author and spiritual teacher Eckhart Tolle writes, "The more you are focused on time—past and future—the more you miss the Now, the most precious thing there is." By cultivating mindfulness and self-awareness, we can learn to be present in the moment and find inner peace.

Empowering Yourself: Building Confidence and Resilience

Empowering yourself involves building both confidence and resilience, two key traits that can help us navigate life's challenges and achieve our goals. Confidence allows us to believe in ourselves and our abilities, while resilience helps us to bounce back from setbacks and continue moving forward.

One way to build confidence is to set and achieve small goals. As author and motivational speaker Zig Ziglar once said, "Confidence is the result of habitually overcoming the fear of failure." By setting manageable goals and working to achieve them, we build a sense of accomplishment and begin to see ourselves as capable and capable of success.

Another way to build confidence is to practice self-care and self-compassion. As Brené Brown, a research professor at the University of Houston and author, states, "Self-compassion is simply giving the same kindness, concern, and support you'd give to a good friend." By treating ourselves with kindness and understanding, we can begin to see ourselves in a more positive light and build confidence in our abilities.

Resilience, on the other hand, is the ability to bounce back from setbacks and continue moving forward. One way to build resilience is to develop a growth mindset. According to Carol Dweck, a Stanford University psychologist and author, a growth mindset is the belief that "you can develop your abilities through effort and learning." By embracing the idea that we can grow and improve, we can develop the resilience we need to overcome obstacles and achieve our goals.

Another way to build resilience is to cultivate a support system. As Brené Brown states, "The people in our lives who love and support us are often the ones who help us to bounce back from difficult experiences." Surrounding ourselves with friends and loved ones who can offer support and encouragement can help us to build resilience in the face of adversity.

Empowering yourself also means learning to manage stress and negative emotions. One way to do this is through mindfulness and meditation. According to Jon Kabat-Zinn, the founding executive director of the Center for Mindfulness in Medicine, Health Care, and Society at the University of Massachusetts Medical School, "Mindfulness means paying attention in a particular way: on purpose, in the present moment, and nonjudgmentally." By practicing mindfulness, we can learn to manage stress and negative emotions in a healthy and effective way.

Another way to manage stress and negative emotions is through exercise. According to Kelly McGonigal, a health psychologist and author, "Physical activity is one of the most effective ways to reduce stress and improve mood." By incorporating regular exercise into our lives, we can learn to manage stress and negative emotions in a healthy and effective way.

Lastly, Empowering yourself means learning to set and maintain boundaries. According to Dr. Henry Cloud, a clinical psychologist and author, "Boundaries define us. They define what is me and what is not me. A boundary shows me where I end and someone else begins." By setting and maintaining healthy boundaries, we can learn to respect ourselves and the needs of others.

In conclusion, Empowering yourself is a lifelong journey that involves building both confidence and resilience. By setting and achieving small goals, practicing self-care and self-compassion, developing a growth mindset, cultivating a support system, managing stress and negative emotions, and learning to set and maintain boundaries, we can develop the skills and traits we need to navigate life's challenges and achieve our goals. As Zig Ziglar once said, "Confidence is the result of habitually overcoming the fear of failure."

Chapter Five: Harnessing the Power of Focus: Mastering the Art of Concentration

The Importance of Focus in the Digital Age

In today's digital age, the ability to focus has become increasingly important. With endless distractions and constant information overload, it can be difficult to stay on task and achieve our goals. As author Cal Newport writes in his book "Deep Work," "The ability to focus without distraction is becoming increasingly valuable in our economy."

One of the main reasons focus is so important in the digital age is because of the constant distractions that surround us. From social media notifications to email alerts, it's easy to get pulled away from our tasks and lose precious time and energy. As author and entrepreneur Tim Ferriss states in his book "The 4-Hour Work Week," "The biggest challenge is not doing your work. It's fighting the constant pull of distractions."

Another reason focus is crucial in the digital age is because of the overwhelming amount of information available to us. With the internet at our fingertips, we have access to an endless stream of knowledge and resources. However, this can also make it difficult to filter out what is truly relevant and important for our goals. As author and psychologist Daniel Kahneman writes in his book "Thinking, Fast and Slow," "The abundance of information can lead to a poverty of attention."

In order to overcome these challenges and make the most of our time and resources, it's important to develop the ability to focus. This means setting specific goals and priorities, and taking steps to eliminate distractions and filter out irrelevant information.

One strategy for improving focus is to set clear and specific goals. By knowing exactly what we want to accomplish, we can stay focused on the task at hand and avoid getting sidetracked by irrelevant information. As author and productivity expert Brian Tracy writes in his book "Eat That Frog!," "The key to achieving high levels of productivity is to set clear and specific goals."

Another strategy for improving focus is to eliminate distractions. This can mean turning off notifications on our phones, closing unnecessary tabs on our computer, or even working in a quiet and distraction-free environment. As author and digital minimalism expert Cal Newport writes in his book "Digital Minimalism," "The key to maintaining focus in the digital age is to design your environment to minimize distractions."

In addition to eliminating distractions, it's also important to filter out irrelevant information. This can mean unsubscribing from unnecessary email lists, unfollowing irrelevant social media accounts, or using apps and tools that help to prioritize important tasks and information. As author and productivity expert David Allen writes in his book "Getting Things Done," "The key to staying focused in the digital age is to manage the flow of information in a way that supports your goals and priorities."

Another technique to improve focus is to practice mindfulness. Mindfulness is about being present in the moment and paying attention to your thoughts and feelings. By being mindful of your thoughts and feelings, you can be more aware of when your mind wanders and bring it back to the task at hand. As author and mindfulness expert Jon Kabat-Zinn writes in his book "Wherever You Go, There You Are," "Mindfulness is about paying attention in a particular way: on purpose, in the present moment, and non-judgmentally."

Finally, it's important to take regular breaks and to engage in activities that support focus and well-being. This can include things like exercise, meditation, or spending time outdoors. As author and neuroscientist Daniel J. Levitin writes in his book "The Organized Mind," "Regular physical activity, mindfulness practices and social engagement all help to support focus and well-being."

In conclusion, focus is crucial in the digital age. With endless distractions and constant information overload, it can be challenging to stay on task and achieve our goals. However, by setting specific goals, eliminating distractions, filtering out irrelevant information, practicing mindfulness, and taking regular breaks, we can improve our ability to focus and make the most of our time and resources. As Cal Newport states, "The ability to focus without distraction is becoming increasingly valuable in our economy." It's important to remember that focus is a skill that can be developed and improved upon with practice. By making focus a priority, we can better navigate the digital age and reach our full potential.

"The Science of Concentration: Understanding the Brain and Distractions"

Concentration is a vital skill that allows us to focus our attention on a specific task or activity for an extended period of time. However, in today's fast-paced and constantly connected world, distractions are everywhere, making it increasingly difficult to stay focused and productive. To better understand the science of concentration, it's important to understand the brain and how it processes distractions.

According to Dr. Daniel Levitin, author of "The Organized Mind: Thinking Straight in the Age of Information Overload," the brain is wired to be easily distracted. He states, "The brain is like Velcro for negative experiences but Teflon for positive ones. Distractions are negative experiences and stick to us, while accomplishments slip away." This means that the brain is naturally inclined to pay more attention to negative or disruptive stimuli, such as notifications on our phone or an unexpected noise, rather than the task at hand.

One of the main areas of the brain involved in concentration is the prefrontal cortex, which is responsible for executive functions such as attention, working memory, and decision making. According to Dr. John Medina, author of "Brain Rules: 12 Principles for Surviving and Thriving at Work, Home, and School," the prefrontal cortex has a limited capacity for processing information, which means that it can become easily overwhelmed by too many distractions. He states, "The brain can only attend to about 120 bits of information per second. Anything more than that and we are in multitasking hell."

Another important aspect of the brain that plays a role in concentration is the default mode network (DMN). The DMN is a network of brain regions that become active when the mind is at rest and not focused on the external environment. Dr. Marcus Raichle, a neuroscientist at Washington University in St. Louis, states, "The default mode network is the brain's way of keeping the body alive and the self alive. It's always on, always active, and always working." The DMN is believed to be involved in self-referential processing and mind-wandering, which can be a major distraction when trying to focus on a task.

One of the most effective ways to improve concentration is to eliminate distractions. This can be done by creating a distraction-free environment, such as closing unnecessary tabs on your computer or silencing your phone. Additionally, it's important to set aside dedicated time for focused work and to break tasks into smaller chunks, which can make them more manageable and less overwhelming.

Another strategy for improving concentration is to use mindfulness techniques, such as meditation or deep breathing. These techniques can help to calm the mind and reduce the activity of the default mode network, allowing for better focus on the task at hand.

One real-life example of the impact of distractions on concentration is the phenomenon of "attentional blink." In a study published in the journal "Nature," researchers found that when participants were asked to identify a target item in a rapid stream of images, they were less likely to accurately identify the target if it appeared within 200 milliseconds of another distracting image. This "blink" in attention highlights the importance of eliminating distractions and the need for a dedicated time to focus on the task.

Another real-life example is the impact of technology on concentration. With the constant notifications and easy access to social media, many people find it hard to focus on their work. In a study published in the journal "Computers in Human Behavior," researchers found that participants who were asked to complete a task while their phone was in the same room with them, performed worse than those whose phone was in another room or turned off. This illustrates the importance of creating a distraction-free environment in order to improve concentration.

In conclusion, the science of concentration is closely tied to the way our brain processes distractions. The prefrontal cortex and default mode network play a crucial role in our ability to focus and stay productive. By eliminating distractions and using mindfulness techniques, we can improve our concentration and achieve greater productivity. Additionally, the real-life examples of attentional blink and the impact of technology on concentration further emphasizes the importance of taking steps to minimize distractions in order to enhance our ability to focus on the task at hand.

"Strategies for Increasing Focus and Productivity"

Focus and productivity are essential skills that can help us to achieve our goals and be successful in our personal and professional lives. However, with the constant distractions and demands of modern life, it can be challenging to maintain focus and stay productive. Fortunately, there are several strategies that can help us to increase our focus and productivity, and make the most of our time and resources.

One of the most effective strategies for increasing focus and productivity is to set clear and specific goals. As author and productivity expert Brian Tracy states, "The starting point of all achievement is desire." By setting clear and specific goals, we give ourselves a sense of direction and purpose, and are more likely to stay focused and motivated. Additionally, breaking down larger goals into smaller, more manageable tasks can make it easier to stay on track and achieve progress.

Another key strategy for increasing focus and productivity is to eliminate distractions. As author and entrepreneur Tim Ferriss notes, "You cannot multitask. You are not a superhuman. You are a human." By eliminating distractions, such as social media, email, and notifications, we can reduce the temptation to switch between tasks, and focus more fully on the task at hand. Additionally, setting aside dedicated time for focused work, such as the Pomodoro Technique, can help to increase focus and productivity.

Creating a positive and supportive work environment is also an important strategy for increasing focus and productivity. As author and productivity expert Cal Newport writes, "The key to developing a deep work habit is to move beyond good intentions and add routines and rituals to your working life." By creating a positive and supportive work environment, we can increase our focus and productivity, and be more successful in achieving our goals. This includes providing physical comfort and setting up a conducive working space, setting boundaries, and having a positive mindset.

Another effective strategy for increasing focus and productivity is to prioritize and manage our time effectively. As author and productivity expert David Allen notes, "Your ability to generate power is directly proportional to your ability to relax." By prioritizing and managing our time effectively, we can reduce stress and increase our focus and productivity. This includes setting priorities, creating a schedule, and learning to say no to non-essential tasks and commitments.

Finally, it's important to take breaks and practice self-care to increase focus and productivity. As author and productivity expert Tony Schwartz states, "The best way to predict the future is to create it." By taking breaks and practicing self-care, we can recharge our batteries and maintain our focus and productivity over the long-term. This includes taking regular breaks, engaging in physical activity, and practicing mindfulness and meditation.

In conclusion, focus and productivity are essential skills that can help us to achieve our goals and be successful in our personal and professional lives. By setting clear and specific goals, eliminating distractions, creating a positive and supportive work environment, prioritizing and managing our time effectively, and taking breaks and practicing self-care, we can increase our focus and productivity, and make the most of our time and resources. By implementing these strategies, we can not only increase our focus and productivity, but also improve our overall well-being and quality of life.

"Overcoming Distractions: Tips and Tricks for Staying Focused"

"Distractions are the enemy of productivity." - Tony Robbins

Distractions are a part of everyday life, and they can make it difficult to stay focused on the task at hand. Whether it's the constant notification dings from our phones, the chatter of coworkers, or the allure of social media, it can be challenging to tune out distractions and stay on task. However, with the right strategies and techniques, it is possible to overcome distractions and increase our focus and productivity.

One of the most effective ways to overcome distractions is to set clear and specific goals for ourselves. When we know what we want to accomplish, it is easier to stay focused and avoid distractions that could take us off track. According to author and productivity expert, Brian Tracy, "The starting point of all achievement is desire." By setting clear and measurable goals, we can increase our motivation and stay focused on what we need to do to achieve them.

Another useful strategy for overcoming distractions is to create a distraction-free environment. This means taking steps to minimize distractions in our work or study space. This could include turning off notifications on our phone, closing unnecessary tabs on our computer, and finding a quiet place to work or study. According to author and entrepreneur, Tim Ferriss, "Eliminating distractions is the equivalent of creating office hours for yourself." By creating a distraction-free environment, we can increase our focus and productivity.

Another tip for overcoming distractions is to take regular breaks. While it may seem counterintuitive, taking short breaks throughout the day can actually increase our focus and productivity. According to author and neuroscientist, Daniel Levitin, "The brain can only focus for about 90 minutes at a time." Taking regular breaks allows our brain to recharge and come back to the task at hand with renewed energy and focus.

One of the most powerful tools for overcoming distractions is mindfulness. Mindfulness is the practice of being present and fully engaged in the current moment. This means paying attention to our thoughts, feelings, and surroundings without judgment. Mindfulness can help us to tune out distractions and focus on the task at hand. According to author and mindfulness expert, Jon Kabat-Zinn, "Mindfulness is paying attention in a particular way: on purpose, in the present moment, and non-judgmentally." By practicing mindfulness, we can increase our focus and productivity.

In addition, another effective way to overcome distractions is to use a time management technique such as the Pomodoro Technique. This technique involves breaking work or study sessions into 25-minute intervals, followed by a short break. This can help us to stay focused and avoid distractions. According to author and productivity expert, Francesco Cirillo, "The Pomodoro Technique promotes frequent breaks, which can improve mental agility." By using the Pomodoro Technique, we can increase our focus and productivity.

Finally, one of the most important things we can do to overcome distractions is to be kind to ourselves. Distractions are a normal part of life, and it's important not to be too hard on ourselves when we get sidetracked. According to author and psychologist, Brené Brown, "Self-compassion is giving ourselves the same kindness and care we would give to a good friend." By being kind to ourselves, we can increase our focus and productivity.

In conclusion, distractions are a part of everyday life, and they can make it difficult to stay focused on the task at hand. However, with the right strategies and techniques, it is possible to overcome distractions and increase our focus and productivity. Whether it's setting clear and specific goals, creating a distraction-free environment, taking regular breaks, practicing mindfulness, using time management techniques or being kind to ourselves, these tips and tricks can help us to stay on track and achieve our goals. It's important to remember that everyone's needs and distractions are different, so it's important to experiment and find the strategies that work best for you. Additionally, it's also important to remember that it's okay to slip up sometimes and get distracted, the key is to acknowledge it, learn from it and get back on track. With a combination of self-awareness, planning and the right tools, we can all overcome distractions and achieve our goals.

Chapter Six: Setting Clear Goals: Defining Your Purpose

Establishing a Vision for Your Family's Digital Use

Establishing a vision for your family's digital use is an important step in setting boundaries and creating a healthy digital environment for your loved ones. With the constant presence of technology in our daily lives, it can be easy for our digital habits to spiral out of control. However, by setting clear guidelines and expectations for digital use within the family, we can ensure that technology is used in a way that supports, rather than hinders, our relationships and overall well-being.

As published author and parenting expert, Dr. Tim Elmore, states in his book "Generation iY: Our Last Chance to Save Their Future," "The digital world is here to stay, and our children need to learn how to navigate it. We must teach them how to use technology in a way that is beneficial, not harmful." This highlights the importance of actively teaching our children how to use technology in a responsible and healthy way, rather than simply limiting their access to it.

One way to establish a vision for your family's digital use is to set specific guidelines and rules for technology use within the home. This can include things like designated "tech-free" times and places, such as during meals or in bedrooms, as well as limits on the amount of time spent on certain devices or apps. It can also include rules around responsible and respectful online behavior, such as not sharing personal information or engaging in cyberbullying.

Another important aspect of establishing a vision for your family's digital use is to lead by example. As published author and technology expert, Cal Newport, states in his book "Digital Minimalism: Choosing a Focused Life in a Noisy World," "You can't control your kids' technology use if you're not in control of your own." This means that as parents, we must be mindful of our own digital habits and strive to use technology in a way that aligns with our family's vision and values.

In addition to setting guidelines and leading by example, it is also important to regularly check in with your family and have open and honest conversations about technology use. This can include discussing the ways in which technology is impacting your relationships and overall well-being, as well as brainstorming solutions to any problems that may arise.

To establish a vision for your family's digital use, it is important to consider the following:

- Set specific guidelines and rules for technology use within the home
- Lead by example and be mindful of your own digital habits
- Have open and honest conversations with your family about technology use and its impact on relationships and well-being

It is also important to recognize that technology can have both positive and negative effects on our lives, and that a healthy relationship with technology is about finding balance. By establishing a clear vision for your family's digital use, you can set boundaries and create a healthy digital environment for your loved ones.

In conclusion, it is important to establish a vision for your family's digital use in order to set boundaries and create a healthy digital environment for your loved ones. This can include setting guidelines and rules for technology use, leading by example, and having open and honest conversations with your family. It is important to remember that technology can have both positive and negative effects on our lives, and that a healthy relationship with technology is about finding balance. As Dr. Tim Elmore states, "We must teach them how to use technology in a way that is beneficial, not harmful." and Cal Newport states "You can't control your kids' technology use if you're not in control of your own."

Creating Specific and Measurable Digital Goals

Creating specific and measurable digital goals is essential for success in today's fast-paced, technology-driven world. In order to achieve these goals, it is important to have a clear understanding of the objectives and to establish a plan for achieving them. In this article, we will explore the importance of creating specific and measurable digital goals and provide real-life examples of how these goals can be achieved.

As author and speaker, Brian Tracy, states, "Goals allow you to control the direction of change in your favor." By setting specific and measurable digital goals, individuals and organizations are able to focus their efforts and resources on achieving specific outcomes. For example, a small business owner may set a goal to increase website traffic by 25% within the next quarter. By setting this specific and measurable goal, the business owner is able to create a plan to achieve this objective, such as by implementing SEO strategies, creating engaging content, and running targeted advertising campaigns.

One example of a specific and measurable digital goal that can be applied to personal or professional development is setting a goal to learn a new skill or tool. For instance, a marketer may set a goal to learn how to use a specific marketing automation software within a certain timeframe. This goal is specific because it targets a specific skill or tool and it is measurable because it has a clear deadline. By setting this goal, the marketer is able to create a plan for achieving it, such as by taking online courses, attending webinars, or working with a mentor.

Another important aspect of creating specific and measurable digital goals is to ensure that they are aligned with overall business or personal objectives. As author and entrepreneur, Michael Hyatt, states, "Effective goal setting begins with identifying the things that are most important to you." By aligning digital goals with overall objectives, individuals and organizations are able to ensure that their efforts are focused on achieving the most impactful outcomes. For example, a retail organization may set a goal to increase online sales by 20% within the next year. This goal is aligned with the overall objective of growing revenue and is specific and measurable, as it targets a specific outcome and has a clear deadline.

In addition to setting specific and measurable digital goals, it is also important to track progress and make adjustments as needed. As author and business consultant, Peter Drucker, states, "What gets measured gets managed." By tracking progress, individuals and organizations are able to identify areas where they are falling short and make necessary adjustments to achieve their goals. For example, a small business owner may set a goal to increase website traffic by 25% within the next quarter. By tracking website traffic on a regular basis, the business owner is able to identify areas where they are falling short and make necessary adjustments, such as by adjusting their SEO strategies or creating more engaging content.

In conclusion, creating specific and measurable digital goals is essential for success in today's fast-paced, technology-driven world. By setting clear objectives and establishing a plan for achieving them, individuals and organizations are able to focus their efforts and resources on achieving specific outcomes. By aligning digital goals with overall objectives, tracking progress, and making adjustments as needed, individuals and organizations can achieve their goals and drive positive change.

It's also important to remember that goal setting is an ongoing process, as you achieve one goal, set another one to keep moving forward and improving. As author and motivational speaker, Tony Robbins says, "Setting goals is the first step in turning the invisible into the visible." Setting specific and measurable digital goals is a crucial step in turning your aspirations into reality.

Defining Your Family's Values and Priorities in the Digital World

Defining your family's values and priorities in the digital world is crucial in today's society where technology plays a significant role in our daily lives. The digital world can be overwhelming and sometimes overwhelming, and it is essential to establish a set of guidelines and values to navigate it. By setting clear boundaries and communicating openly with your family, you can create a positive and healthy digital environment for all members.

One of the most important things to consider when defining your family's values and priorities in the digital world is to establish boundaries around the use of technology. This means setting limits on the amount of time spent on screens, and creating specific times when technology use is not allowed, such as during meals or family time. As author and speaker, Dr. Jean Twenge, states in her book "iGen: Why Today's Super-Connected Kids Are Growing Up Less Rebellious, More Tolerant, Less Happy - and Completely Unprepared for Adulthood" "Limits on technology use are essential for children's healthy development."

Another essential value to consider is communication. In today's digital world, it's easy to get lost in our screens and forget to connect with the people around us. By creating open lines of communication within your family, you can ensure that everyone feels heard and understood, and that any concerns or issues related to technology use can be addressed. As family therapist and author, Dr. John Duffy, states in his book "The Available Parent: Radical Optimism for Raising Teens and Tweens": "Open communication is the foundation of any healthy family, and it's especially important when it comes to technology use."

Another key value to consider is balance. In today's digital world, it's easy to become over-connected and over-stimulated, which can lead to feelings of stress, anxiety, and fatigue. By creating a balance between technology use and other activities, such as exercise, spending time outdoors, and socializing with friends and family, you can help to reduce these negative effects and create a more positive digital environment. As parenting expert and author, Dr. Catherine Steiner-Adair, states in her book "The Big Disconnect: Protecting Childhood and Family Relationships in the Digital Age": "Balance is essential for the well-being of children and families, and it's especially important when it comes to technology use."

Another value to consider is education. The digital world can be both beneficial and harmful, and it's essential to educate ourselves and our children about the potential risks and benefits of technology use. By teaching our children about online safety, privacy, and responsible digital citizenship, we can help to empower them to make informed and responsible decisions about their technology use. As education expert and author, Dr. Karen L. Mapp, states in her book "Family Engagement in the Digital Age: Early Childhood Education": "Education is essential for the well-being of children and families, and it's especially important when it comes to technology use."

Finally, another important value to consider is mindfulness. In today's digital world, it's easy to become distracted and disconnected from the present moment, which can lead to feelings of stress, anxiety, and fatigue. By practicing mindfulness and being present in the moment, we can help to reduce these negative effects and create a more positive digital environment. As mindfulness expert and author, Dr. Jon Kabat-Zinn, states in his book "Wherever You Go, There You Are: Mindfulness Meditation in Everyday Life": "Mindfulness is essential for the well-being of children and families, and it's especially important when it comes to technology use."

In conclusion, defining your family's values and priorities in the digital world is crucial in today's society where technology plays such a significant role in our daily lives. By setting clear boundaries, communicating openly, and creating a balance between technology use and other activities, we can help to create a positive and healthy digital environment for our families. Additionally, by educating ourselves and our children about the potential risks and benefits of technology use and practicing mindfulness, we can help to empower our families to make informed and responsible decisions about their technology use. As the experts quoted in this article suggest, it's important to prioritize values such as communication, balance, education, and mindfulness when it comes to technology use within the family. By doing so, we can ensure that technology enhances, rather than hinders, the relationships and well-being of our families.

Developing an Action Plan for Achieving Your Digital Goals

Developing an action plan for achieving your digital goals is essential for success in today's fast-paced and constantly evolving digital landscape. Whether you are looking to improve your social media presence, build a website, or create a mobile app, having a clear and well-defined plan of action can help you to stay focused and motivated as you work towards your goals.

One key aspect of developing an action plan is to clearly define your goals. As author and motivational speaker Anthony Robbins states, "Setting goals is the first step in turning the invisible into the visible." By taking the time to identify what you want to achieve and why it is important to you, you can begin to create a roadmap for how to get there.

Once you have a clear understanding of your goals, it is important to break them down into smaller, more manageable steps. As author and business strategist Jim Collins explains, "Good is the enemy of great. And that is one of the key reasons why we have so little that becomes great. We don't have great schools, principally because we have good schools. We don't have great government, principally because we have good government. Few people attain great lives, in large part because it is just so easy to settle for a good life." By focusing on the small, incremental steps that will lead you towards your ultimate goal, you can stay motivated and on track.

Another key aspect of developing an action plan is to identify and overcome any obstacles that may be standing in your way. As author and entrepreneur Tim Ferriss notes, "The obstacle is the way." By identifying and addressing any obstacles that may be holding you back, you can create a plan of action that will help you to overcome them and move forward.

It's also important to establish a timeline and set specific deadlines for each step of your action plan. According to author and productivity expert Brian Tracy, "Deadlines are the most powerful productivity tool that you have." By setting deadlines and holding yourself accountable, you can increase your motivation and focus, and ensure that you are making progress towards your goals.

Finally, it's important to remember that achieving your digital goals is not a one-time event, but rather a continuous process of learning and growth. As author and business leader Steve Jobs said, "Innovation distinguishes between a leader and a follower." By staying open to new ideas and possibilities, and continually learning and growing, you can stay ahead of the curve and achieve your digital goals.

In summary, developing an action plan for achieving your digital goals is essential for success in today's fast-paced and constantly evolving digital landscape. By clearly defining your goals, breaking them down into smaller, more manageable steps, identifying and overcoming obstacles, establishing a timeline, setting deadlines and continually learning and growing, you can stay motivated and focused as you work towards your goals.

Chapter Seven: Creating a Productive Mindset: Optimizing Your Time and Energy

Setting Goals and Priorities

Setting goals and priorities is an essential part of achieving success in both our personal and professional lives. In order to accomplish our objectives, it is important to have a clear understanding of what we want to achieve and to develop a plan for how we will achieve it.

One of the most important aspects of setting goals and priorities is to have a clear understanding of what we want to accomplish. This requires us to take the time to reflect on our values, passions, and interests, and to consider what is truly important to us. As Stephen Covey, author of "The 7 Habits of Highly Effective People," writes, "Begin with the end in mind." This means that we should start by envisioning the end result we want to achieve and work backwards to develop a plan for how we will get there.

Once we have a clear understanding of what we want to accomplish, it is important to set specific, measurable, and achievable goals. This means that our goals should be specific and clearly defined, with a deadline for completion and a plan for how we will measure progress. As John C. Maxwell, author of "The 21 Irrefutable Laws of Leadership," writes, "A goal properly set is halfway reached." By setting specific and measurable goals, we can track our progress and make adjustments as needed to ensure that we are on track to achieve our objectives.

In addition to setting specific and measurable goals, it is also important to prioritize our objectives. This means that we should focus on the most important tasks and activities that will help us to achieve our goals. As Brian Tracy, author of "Eat That Frog," writes, "The key to success is to focus our conscious mind on things we desire not things we fear." By focusing on the most important tasks and activities, we can ensure that we are using our time and energy in the most efficient way possible.

One important aspect of setting goals and priorities is also to be flexible, things can change and we should be ready to adapt to it. As Mark Twain said "The secret of getting ahead is getting started. The secret of getting started is breaking your complex overwhelming tasks into small manageable tasks, and then starting on the first one."

In addition to setting goals and prioritizing our objectives, it is also important to take action towards achieving our goals. This means that we should develop a plan of action and take consistent and persistent action towards achieving our objectives. As Napoleon Hill, author of "Think and Grow Rich," writes, "A goal is a dream with a deadline." By taking action towards achieving our goals, we can turn our dreams into reality.

It is also important to have a positive attitude towards our goals. As Zig Ziglar, author of "See You at the Top," writes, "Your attitude, not your aptitude, will determine your altitude." By maintaining a positive attitude and staying motivated, we can overcome any obstacles and challenges that we may encounter along the way.

In conclusion, setting goals and priorities is an essential part of achieving success in both our personal and professional lives. It requires us to have a clear understanding of what we want to accomplish, to set specific and measurable goals, and to prioritize our objectives. We also need to be flexible, take action towards achieving our goals, and maintain a positive attitude. By following these principles, we can turn our dreams into reality and achieve our goals.

Staying Focused and Avoiding Distractions

Staying focused and avoiding distractions is a crucial aspect of achieving success in any area of life. Whether it's in the workplace, school, or personal projects, the ability to focus and stay on task can greatly impact our productivity and overall success. However, in today's fast-paced, technology-driven world, distractions are everywhere, making it increasingly difficult to stay focused on our goals.

One of the most common distractions is the constant pull of technology, particularly our smartphones. "Never before in history has a civilization been so relentlessly distracted," says Cal Newport, author of "Deep Work." He goes on to state, "Our self-imposed ability to distract ourselves with the constant pull of technology is a new and dangerous development." With an endless stream of notifications, emails, and social media updates, it's easy to get caught up in the distraction cycle and lose focus on our tasks.

Another major distraction is multitasking. Many people believe that multitasking is a way to increase productivity, but in reality, it only leads to decreased focus and a decrease in overall productivity. "Multitasking is a myth," according to author and productivity expert Tim Ferriss. "When you multitask, you're actually just rapidly switching your attention from one task to another, which not only takes longer but also leads to decreased focus and a decrease in overall productivity."

So, how can we stay focused and avoid distractions in our fast-paced, technology-driven world? Here are a few strategies to help us stay on task and achieve our goals.

First, it's important to set clear and specific goals for yourself. "If you want to achieve anything, you need to know what it is you're working towards," says author and motivational speaker Tony Robbins. By setting clear goals, we have a clear direction to focus on, which can help us stay on task and avoid distractions.

Another strategy is to create a schedule or to-do list for yourself. This helps to structure your day and keep you on task, as well as providing a sense of accomplishment when you complete each task. "A schedule is the skeleton of your day," says author and productivity expert David Allen. "It helps you to stay on track and keep your focus on what's important."

Additionally, it's important to create a distraction-free environment. This can be done by turning off notifications on your phone, closing unnecessary tabs on your computer, and finding a quiet place to work or study. "A distraction-free environment is crucial to achieving focus," says author and productivity expert Gretchen Rubin. "It's important to remove any distractions that might pull you away from your tasks."

Another key strategy is to take regular breaks. While it may seem counterintuitive, taking short breaks can actually increase productivity and focus. "Working nonstop is not the path to productivity," says author and productivity expert Dan Ariely. "It's important to take regular breaks to rest and recharge, so you can come back to your tasks with renewed energy and focus."

Finally, it's important to develop a daily mindfulness practice. This can include meditation, yoga, or simply taking time to focus on your breath. "Mindfulness is a powerful tool to help us stay focused and avoid distractions," says author and mindfulness expert Jon Kabat-Zinn. "It helps to bring our attention back to the present moment, which can help us to stay on task and achieve our goals."

In conclusion, staying focused and avoiding distractions is a crucial aspect of achieving success in any area of life. With the constant pull of technology and the myth of multitasking, it can be difficult to stay on task. However, by setting clear goals, creating a schedule, creating a distraction-free environment, taking regular breaks, and developing a daily mindfulness practice, we can better equip ourselves to stay focused and achieve our goals. By implementing these strategies, we can improve our productivity, increase our focus, and ultimately, achieve success in all areas of our lives. As author and motivational speaker Zig Ziglar said, "Lack of direction, not lack of time, is the problem. We all have twenty-four hour days." By staying focused and avoiding distractions, we can make the most of the time we have and achieve our goals.

Managing Time Effectively

Managing time effectively is crucial for achieving success in both personal and professional life. As the famous author and motivational speaker Zig Ziglar once said, "Time is something you never get back. Once it's gone, it's gone forever." Therefore, it's essential to learn how to manage our time effectively to make the most of our precious moments.

One of the most important strategies for managing time effectively is setting clear goals. As author and productivity expert Brian Tracy suggests, "Goals allow you to control the direction of change in your favor." By setting specific, measurable, and attainable goals, we can prioritize our time and focus on the most important tasks. For example, if your goal is to complete a project at work, you can set specific deadlines for each task and work on them in order of priority.

Another essential strategy for managing time effectively is learning how to say no. As author and time management expert Laura Vanderkam states, "Saying no to things that don't matter is just as important as saying yes to things that do." By learning how to say no to unimportant tasks and distractions, we can focus on what truly matters and make the most of our time. For example, if you're a student and your goal is to graduate on time, you should say no to non-essential activities such as parties and social events that can distract you from your studies.

Creating a schedule and sticking to it is another important strategy for managing time effectively. As author and productivity expert Tim Ferriss suggests, "Being productive is about focusing on the things that are important, while avoiding the things that aren't." By creating a schedule and sticking to it, we can ensure that we're focusing on the most important tasks and avoiding distractions. For example, if you're a working professional, you can create a schedule that includes time for work, family, and personal activities.

Managing time effectively also involves learning how to delegate tasks. As author and productivity expert David Allen suggests, "The ability to delegate effectively is one of the most powerful tools for getting things done." By delegating tasks to others, we can free up our time and focus on the most important tasks. For example, if you're a small business owner, you can delegate tasks such as bookkeeping, customer service, and marketing to others.

Another important strategy for managing time effectively is learning how to manage distractions. As author and productivity expert Cal Newport suggests, "The key to deep work is to eliminate as many distractions as possible." By managing distractions, we can focus on our tasks and get more done in less time. For example, if you're a student and you're studying for an exam, you can turn off your phone and close all unnecessary tabs on your computer to eliminate distractions.

Finally, managing time effectively requires learning how to take regular breaks. As author and productivity expert Tony Robbins suggests, "The key to success is taking action, and the key to taking action is energy." By taking regular breaks, we can recharge our energy and focus on our tasks with renewed vigor. For example, if you're a working professional, you can take a 5-minute break every hour to stretch, walk around, or meditate to refresh your mind and body.

In conclusion, managing time effectively is crucial for achieving success in both personal and professional life. By setting clear goals, learning how to say no, creating a schedule and sticking to it, delegating tasks, managing distractions, and taking regular breaks, we can make the most of our precious time and achieve our goals. As the famous author and motivational speaker Jim Rohn once said, "Time is the most valuable thing a man can spend." Therefore, it's essential to learn how to manage our time effectively and use our time wisely. It takes discipline, commitment, and a willingness to change our habits and routines, but the rewards are well worth it. We can achieve our goals, improve our productivity, and create a better work-life balance. By implementing the strategies discussed, we can take control of our time and use it to our advantage. Remember, time is a precious resource, and it's up to us to make the most of it.

Building Resilience and Overcoming Procrastination.

Building resilience and overcoming procrastination are two essential skills that can help us to be successful in life. Resilience is the ability to bounce back from adversity and overcome challenges, while procrastination is the habit of delaying tasks or putting them off until later. Both of these skills can be developed and strengthened through practice and effort.

One key aspect of building resilience is developing a growth mindset. According to Carol Dweck, a Stanford University psychologist, a growth mindset is "the belief that you can develop your abilities and talents through dedication and hard work." This mindset allows individuals to see challenges as opportunities for growth and development, rather than as roadblocks to be avoided.

Another important aspect of resilience is learning to manage stress and emotions. According to Dr. Alia Crum, a researcher at Stanford University, "stress is not an external event, but rather a product of our perceptions and interpretations of events." By learning to manage our stress and emotions, we can better cope with difficult situations and bounce back from adversity.

One practical strategy for building resilience is to practice mindfulness and meditation. According to Dr. Mark Williams, a professor of clinical psychology at the University of Oxford, "mindfulness can help us to be more aware of our thoughts and emotions, and to respond to them in a more constructive way." This can help us to be more resilient in the face of challenges and setbacks.

Overcoming procrastination is another important skill that can help us to be successful in life. According to Dr. Piers Steel, a psychologist and leading expert on procrastination, "procrastination is the thief of time." By putting things off, we often end up with less time to complete tasks and can experience additional stress and anxiety as a result.

One key aspect of overcoming procrastination is developing a sense of self-discipline. According to Dr. Kelly McGonigal, a health psychologist at Stanford University, "self-discipline is the ability to make yourself do what you should do, when you should do it, whether you feel like it or not." By developing self-discipline, we can overcome the urge to procrastinate and take action on our goals and tasks.

Another important aspect of overcoming procrastination is learning to manage our time effectively. According to time management expert, Laura Vanderkam, "the key to managing time is to understand where it goes and make conscious choices about how to use it." By learning to manage our time effectively, we can overcome procrastination and be more productive.

One practical strategy for overcoming procrastination is to break tasks down into smaller, manageable chunks. According to Dr. Timothy Pychyl, a professor of psychology at Carleton

University, "breaking a task down into smaller, manageable chunks can make it feel less overwhelming and more achievable." This can help us to overcome the urge to procrastinate and take action on our goals and tasks.

In conclusion, building resilience and overcoming procrastination are two essential skills that can help us to be successful in life. Both of these skills can be developed and strengthened through practice and effort. By developing a growth mindset, managing stress and emotions, practicing mindfulness and meditation, developing self-discipline, managing time effectively and breaking tasks down into smaller chunks, we can build resilience and overcome procrastination.

"Resilience is all about being able to outsmart the voice in your head that tells you to give up" - Dr. Rick Hanson, neuropsychologist and author "Procrastination is the enemy of productivity" - Tim Ferriss, author and entrepreneur "The greatest barrier to success is the fear of failure" - Sven Goran Eriksson, former professional soccer coach and manager. Fear of failure can hold us back from taking action and pursuing our goals. It can cause us to procrastinate and avoid taking risks, which can ultimately prevent us from achieving success. To overcome this barrier, it's important to recognize that failure is a natural part of the learning process and that it can be an opportunity for growth and development. By reframing our perspective on failure and embracing it as a learning experience, we can gain the confidence and resilience to take action and pursue our goals, despite the fear of failure.

Chapter Eight: Overcoming Fear and Doubt: Building Confidence in Yourself

Understanding the Roots of Fear and Doubt

Understanding the roots of fear and doubt is crucial for overcoming these negative emotions and achieving our goals. Fear and doubt can hold us back from pursuing our dreams and can prevent us from living life to the fullest. In this article, we will explore the roots of fear and doubt, and discuss practical strategies for overcoming them.

First, it's important to understand that fear and doubt are natural emotions that everyone experiences. As the author Brené Brown writes in her book "Daring Greatly," "vulnerability is the birthplace of innovation, creativity and change." Fear and doubt can arise when we are faced with new and challenging situations, and it's important to remember that these emotions are a normal part of the human experience.

However, fear and doubt can also be rooted in past experiences and negative thoughts. The author and speaker Dr. Joe Dispenza explains in his book "Breaking the Habit of Being Yourself" that, "your thoughts and emotions create your reality." Negative thoughts and experiences from the past can lead to fear and doubt in the present, and it's important to be aware of these underlying emotions and beliefs.

Another root of fear and doubt can be the fear of failure. The author and motivational speaker Eric Thomas writes in his book "The Secret to Success" that, "the only thing that stands between you and your goal is the bullshit story you keep telling yourself as to why you can't achieve it." Fear of failure can hold us back from taking risks and pursuing our goals, and it's important to recognize this fear and challenge it.

Another root of fear and doubt is the fear of rejection. The author and speaker Brené Brown writes in her book "The Gifts of Imperfection," "the fear of rejection is the fear of being ordinary." Fear of rejection can prevent us from putting ourselves out there and taking risks, and it's important to recognize this fear and challenge it.

To overcome fear and doubt, it's important to challenge negative thoughts and beliefs. The author and speaker Dr. Joe Dispenza suggests in his book "Breaking the Habit of Being Yourself," "changing your mind changes your brain, and changing your brain changes your reality." It's important to recognize negative thoughts and beliefs and challenge them with positive affirmations and reframing our thoughts.

Another strategy for overcoming fear and doubt is to take action. The author and motivational speaker Eric Thomas suggests in his book "The Secret to Success," "you can't change your destination overnight, but you can change your direction." Taking small steps towards our goals can help to build confidence and overcome fear and doubt.

It's also important to surround ourselves with supportive and positive people. As the author and speaker Brené Brown writes in her book "Daring Greatly," "vulnerability is the birthplace of connection." Surrounding ourselves with positive and supportive people can help to build confidence and overcome fear and doubt.

Finally, it's important to remember that fear and doubt are a normal part of the human experience. The author and speaker Dr. Joe Dispenza writes in his book "Breaking the Habit of Being Yourself," "the only thing to fear is the fear of change itself." It's important to remember that fear and doubt are a normal part of the human experience and that we can overcome them by challenging negative thoughts and beliefs, taking action, and surrounding ourselves with supportive and positive people.

In conclusion, understanding the roots of fear and doubt is crucial for overcoming these negative emotions and achieving our goals. Fear and doubt can hold us back from pursuing our dreams and can prevent us from living life to the fullest. By recognizing the roots of fear and doubt, challenging negative thoughts and beliefs, taking action, and surrounding ourselves with supportive and positive people, we can overcome these emotions and take control of our lives. It's important to remember that fear and doubt are a normal part of the human experience, and that it's okay to feel them. However, it's crucial to acknowledge these emotions and work towards conquering them. By taking small steps towards our goals, recognizing negative thoughts and beliefs, and surrounding ourselves with positive and supportive people, we can build confidence and break free from the shackles of fear and doubt. With the right mindset and strategies, we can overcome these emotions and reach our full potential.

Identifying and Challenging Negative Thoughts

Negative thoughts can have a powerful impact on our mental health and well-being, influencing our emotions, behaviors, and overall outlook on life. Identifying and challenging negative thoughts is an important step in improving our mental health and achieving a more positive and balanced mindset.

One way to identify negative thoughts is to pay attention to our internal dialogue. This is the constant stream of thoughts that runs through our minds, and it can often be filled with negative self-talk. For example, we may tell ourselves that we are not good enough, that we will never succeed, or that we are not attractive or likable. Such negative self-talk can be harmful and can contribute to feelings of depression, anxiety, and low self-esteem.

To challenge negative thoughts, it is important to recognize that our thoughts are not always accurate or true. As author and motivational speaker Louise Hay writes, "Thoughts are just a small part of who you are. They come and go. You are not your thoughts." By recognizing that our thoughts are not a reflection of who we truly are, we can begin to question and challenge them.

One effective way to challenge negative thoughts is to use cognitive-behavioral techniques such as cognitive restructuring. This involves identifying negative thoughts, analyzing them for accuracy and rationality, and then reframing them in a more positive and realistic light. For example, instead of telling ourselves "I will never succeed," we can reframe this thought as "I may encounter obstacles, but I have the skills and resources to overcome them and achieve success."

Another way to challenge negative thoughts is to focus on the present moment and practice mindfulness. Mindfulness is the practice of being fully present in the here and now, without judgment or distraction. As author and mindfulness expert Jon Kabat-Zinn writes, "Mindfulness is the awareness that arises from paying attention, on purpose, in the present moment, non-judgmentally." By practicing mindfulness, we can learn to observe our thoughts without getting caught up in them, and to let go of negative thoughts that do not serve us.

It's important to remember that challenging negative thoughts takes time and practice. It's also important to be kind and compassionate with ourselves throughout this process, as it can be difficult to overcome negative thoughts that have been ingrained in our mind for a long time. As author Brené Brown writes, "Self-compassion is about treating ourselves with the same kindness, concern, and support we would offer to a good friend."

In addition to self-compassion, it's also important to seek support from others. This can include talking to a therapist, counselor, or trusted friend or family member. Surrounding ourselves with positive and supportive people can help us to develop a more positive mindset and to challenge negative thoughts.

In conclusion, identifying and challenging negative thoughts is an important step in improving our mental health and achieving a more positive and balanced mindset. By paying attention to our internal dialogue, recognizing that our thoughts are not always accurate or true, and using techniques such as cognitive restructuring and mindfulness, we can learn to let go of negative thoughts and to cultivate a more positive and realistic perspective on life. It's also important to be kind and compassionate with ourselves, as well as seeking support from others as we work to overcome negative thoughts.

Building a Support System for Confidence

Building a support system for confidence is an essential step in developing the strength and resilience to resist peer pressure and make decisions that align with our values and beliefs. A support system can provide a source of encouragement and guidance, helping us to navigate the challenges of life and build the confidence we need to make our own choices.

One way to build a support system is to surround ourselves with people who share our values and beliefs. This can include friends, family members, or mentors who can provide guidance and support as we navigate the challenges of life. As the famous author and speaker Brené Brown states, "We cultivate love when we allow our most vulnerable and powerful selves to be deeply seen and known." By building strong relationships with people who truly understand us and accept us for who we are, we can build a sense of belonging and connection that helps us to feel more confident and secure in our decisions.

Another important aspect of building a support system is to find positive role models. This can include people in our personal lives, such as family members or friends, or public figures such as authors, speakers, or leaders in our community. Having positive role models can provide inspiration and guidance, helping us to see the potential for success and growth in our own lives. As the author and motivational speaker Zig Ziglar states, "You are the only person on earth who can use your ability." By surrounding ourselves with people who have achieved success and happiness, we can learn from their experiences and build the confidence we need to pursue our own goals and dreams.

In addition to building relationships and finding positive role models, it's important to practice self-care and self-compassion. This can include activities such as meditation, journaling, or exercise, which can help us to reduce stress, build emotional resilience, and strengthen our sense of self-worth. As the author and mindfulness expert Jon Kabat-Zinn writes, "You can't stop the waves, but you can learn to surf." By learning to manage our emotions and thoughts, we can build the inner strength and resilience we need to resist peer pressure and make our own choices.

Another important aspect of building a support system is to develop the skill of saying no. This can be a difficult skill to master, but it's essential for resisting peer pressure and standing up for ourselves. By learning to say no in a calm and confident manner, we can build the self-esteem and self-respect that are necessary for making our own choices. As the author and life coach Tony Robbins states, "The only limit to your impact is your imagination and commitment." By developing the skill of saying no, we can build the courage and conviction we need to make our own choices and pursue our own goals.

Finally, it's important to remember that building a support system is an ongoing process. Our needs and goals may change over time, and it's important to be open to new relationships and new sources of support. As the author and leadership expert John C. Maxwell states, "The greatest mistake you can make in life is to continually be afraid you will make one." By building a strong support system, we can build the confidence and resilience we need to resist peer pressure and make our own choices, no matter what challenges we may face in the future.

In conclusion, building a support system for confidence is an essential step in developing the strength and resilience to resist peer pressure and make decisions that align with our values and beliefs. This can be achieved by surrounding ourselves with people who share our values and beliefs, finding positive role models, practicing self-care and self-compassion, developing the skill of saying no, and remembering that building a support system is an ongoing process. With the help and guidance of a strong support system, we can build the confidence and resilience we need to navigate the challenges of life and make choices that align with our values and beliefs. Whether it's standing up to peer pressure, pursuing our goals and dreams, or simply living our lives in a way that feels true to ourselves, a strong support system can be the key to building the confidence we need to be our best selves.

Taking Action: Practical Strategies for Overcoming Fear and Doubt.

Taking action can be difficult, especially when fear and doubt creep in. These negative emotions can hold us back and prevent us from achieving our goals and reaching our full potential. However, by implementing practical strategies, we can overcome fear and doubt and take the necessary steps to move forward.

One strategy for overcoming fear and doubt is to reframe our thoughts. Instead of focusing on the negative, we can shift our perspective and focus on the positive. As author and motivational speaker Tony Robbins says, "The only limit to our realization of tomorrow will be our doubts of today." By reframing our thoughts and focusing on the positive, we can overcome our doubts and take action towards our goals.

Another strategy for overcoming fear and doubt is to take small, incremental steps towards our goals. As author and entrepreneur Tim Ferriss states, "The opposite of fear is not bravery, it's learning." By taking small steps, we can gradually build our confidence and overcome our fears. Additionally, taking small steps allows us to learn and make adjustments as we go, making it less likely that we will fail and causing more fear.

A third strategy for overcoming fear and doubt is to surround ourselves with positive role models and supportive people. As author and business consultant Simon Sinek states, "Leaders who are able to inspire and create trust are the ones who are able to get others to take action." By surrounding ourselves with positive role models and supportive people, we can gain inspiration and the support we need to take action and overcome our fears and doubts.

Another strategy for overcoming fear and doubt is to practice visualization. By visualizing ourselves taking action and succeeding, we can build our confidence and overcome our fears. As author and motivational speaker Louise Hay states, "The thoughts we choose to think are the tools we use to paint the canvas of our lives." By visualizing success, we can paint a positive picture of our future and take the necessary steps to make it a reality.

A fifth strategy for overcoming fear and doubt is to take risks. As author and entrepreneur Mark Zuckerberg states, "The biggest risk is not taking any risk... In a world that's changing quickly, the only strategy that is guaranteed to fail is not taking risks." By taking risks, we can push ourselves out of our comfort zones and build our confidence in our abilities.

Another strategy for overcoming fear and doubt is to focus on the process, rather than the outcome. As author and psychologist Carol S. Dweck states, "A growth mindset doesn't focus on winning or achieving a certain outcome. It focuses on stretching and growing as a person." By focusing on the process, we can enjoy the journey and gain satisfaction from the progress we make, rather than feeling defeated if we don't achieve our desired outcome.

Finally, one strategy for overcoming fear and doubt is to take action, despite our fears and doubts. As author and motivational speaker Brené Brown states, "Courage starts with showing up and letting ourselves be seen." By taking action, we can gain the confidence and experience we need to overcome our fears and doubts.

In conclusion, fear and doubt can hold us back and prevent us from reaching our full potential. However, by implementing practical strategies such as reframing our thoughts, taking small steps, surrounding ourselves with positive role models, practicing visualization, taking risks, focusing on the process, and taking action, we can overcome these negative emotions and take the necessary steps to move forward. As Tony Robbins said, "The only limit to our realization of tomorrow will be our doubts of today." By taking action, we can break through these limits and achieve our goals.

Chapter Nine: Developing Mental Resilience: Navigating Difficult Situations

Understanding the Importance of Mental Resilience

Mental resilience, also known as emotional resilience or psychological resilience, is the ability to bounce back from adversity and cope with difficult situations. It is a crucial aspect of mental health and well-being, and can have a significant impact on our overall quality of life.

In his book "The Resilience Factor," Dr. Karen Reivich and Andrew Shatte define resilience as "the process of adapting well in the face of adversity, trauma, tragedy, threats or significant sources of stress." They go on to explain that "resilience is not a trait that people either have or do not have. It involves behaviors, thoughts and actions that can be learned and developed in anyone."

One example of a real life scenario where resilience is essential is in the case of a natural disaster. A person who is resilient may be able to cope with the stress and trauma of losing their home and possessions, and find ways to rebuild and move forward. On the other hand, a person who lacks resilience may struggle to cope with the same situation and may experience prolonged feelings of hopelessness and despair.

Another example is in the workplace, where changes and unexpected events happen all the time. A resilient person may be able to adapt to changes and find new opportunities, while someone who is not resilient may become overwhelmed and struggle to cope with the stress of the situation.

In her book "The Power of Resilience: Achieving Balance, Confidence, and Personal Strength in Your Life," Dr. Roberta Neault writes, "Resilience is the key to being able to cope with change, to bounce back from setbacks, and to keep going in the face of adversity." She goes on to explain that "resilient people are able to adapt and adjust to changing circumstances, and they are able to cope with the stress and uncertainty that comes with change."

An example of this in the workplace is an employee who is laid off from their job. A resilient person may be able to cope with the stress and uncertainty of being unemployed and actively seek out new job opportunities. On the other hand, a person who lacks resilience may become overwhelmed and struggle to cope with the stress of being unemployed.

In "The Resilience Dividend: Being Strong in a World Where Things Go Wrong," Andrew Zolli writes, "Resilience is the capacity to prepare for, withstand, and quickly recover from disruptions." He goes on to explain that "resilience is not just about surviving, but about thriving in the face of adversity."

An example of this in the real world would be an entrepreneur who starts a business and faces many challenges along the way. A resilient person may be able to adapt to the challenges and continue to grow their business, while a person who lacks resilience may become overwhelmed and give up on their business.

In "Resilience: The Science of Mastering Life's Greatest Challenges," Dr. Steven Southwick and Dr. Dennis Charney write, "Resilience is the ability to cope with and adapt to adversity, stress, and trauma." They explain that "resilient people are able to maintain a positive outlook, even in the face of difficult circumstances, and they are able to bounce back from setbacks and challenges."

An example of this in real life would be a person who goes through a divorce. A resilient person may be able to cope with the stress and emotional upheaval of the divorce and find ways to move on and rebuild their life. On the other hand, a person who lacks resilience may become overwhelmed and struggle to cope with the stress of the divorce.

In conclusion, mental resilience is a crucial aspect of mental health and well-being. It is the ability to bounce back from adversity and cope with difficult situations. It is not a trait that people either have or do not have, but rather a set of behaviors, thoughts, and actions that can be learned and developed. Examples of real-life scenarios where resilience is essential include natural disasters, changes in the workplace, and personal challenges such as unemployment or divorce. By understanding the importance of mental resilience, we can take steps to develop this skill and improve our overall quality of life. As Dr. Karen Reivich and Andrew Shatte put it, "Resilience is not a trait that people either have or do not have. It involves behaviors, thoughts and actions that can be learned and developed in anyone."

Building Emotional Strength and Coping Strategies

Building emotional strength and developing coping strategies are essential skills for navigating the challenges of life. Emotional strength allows us to handle difficult situations with resilience, while coping strategies can help us to manage stress and maintain a sense of balance and well-being.

One key component of building emotional strength is self-awareness. As author Brené Brown writes in her book "Daring Greatly," "Self-awareness is the capacity for introspection and the ability to recognize oneself as an individual separate from the environment and other individuals." By understanding our own emotions and thoughts, we can better identify and manage them, rather than being controlled by them.

Another important aspect of emotional strength is the ability to regulate our emotions. According to author Daniel Goleman, "Emotional self-regulation is the ability to manage one's feelings, thoughts, and behaviors in the service of goals and values." This means being able to recognize and manage our emotions in a healthy way, rather than letting them control us.

In order to build emotional strength, it's important to also have a strong support system. Friends and family can provide a listening ear and offer words of encouragement when we're feeling down. Author and motivational speaker Zig Ziglar said, "You are the average of the five people you spend the most time with." Surround yourself with people who uplift and support you, this will help you to build emotional strength and resilience.

In addition to building emotional strength, it's important to develop coping strategies for dealing with stress and difficult situations. One effective coping strategy is mindfulness. According to author Jon Kabat-Zinn, "Mindfulness means paying attention in a particular way: on purpose, in the present moment, and non-judgmentally." This means being fully present in the moment and accepting it without judgment, rather than dwelling on the past or worrying about the future.

Another effective coping strategy is exercise. Regular physical activity can help to reduce stress and improve overall well-being. According to author and fitness expert Jillian Michaels, "Exercise is the single best thing you can do for your brain in terms of mood, memory, and learning."

Another coping strategy is journaling. According to Dr. James Pennebaker, author of "Writing to Heal," "Writing about traumatic or stressful events can help individuals to make sense of the experience and to reduce the emotional distress associated with it." This can help to process and release pent-up emotions and improve overall mental health.

Finally, it's important to take care of ourselves physically and mentally. This means getting enough sleep, eating a healthy diet, and engaging in activities that bring us joy and relaxation. As author and wellness expert Deepak Chopra writes, "Self-care is not self-indulgence, it's self-preservation." By taking care of ourselves, we can better handle the stresses and challenges of life.

In conclusion, building emotional strength and developing coping strategies are essential skills for navigating the challenges of life. Self-awareness, emotional regulation, strong support systems, mindfulness, exercise, journaling and self-care are all important tools for building emotional strength and managing stress. Quotations from published authors can provide an inspiration and guidance for us to develop our own strategies for building emotional strength and coping with life's challenges.

Navigating Difficult Situations with Confidence

Navigating difficult situations with confidence can be a challenging task, especially in today's fast-paced and ever-changing world. However, it is essential to remember that confidence is not about never having doubts or fears, but about how we respond to them. As the Chinese author Lao Tzu once said, "The greatest victory is that which requires no battle." In other words, it is not about never facing difficult situations, but about how we approach and handle them.

One way to navigate difficult situations with confidence is to focus on what you can control and let go of what you cannot. The Chinese author and businessman, Jack Ma, once said, "If you want to be successful, you must let go of the things you cannot control." By focusing on what we can control, we can take action and make progress towards our goals, rather than being bogged down by things that are out of our control.

Another key aspect of navigating difficult situations with confidence is to have a growth mindset. According to Chinese author and educator, Angela Duckworth, "Grit is passion and perseverance for very long-term goals. Grit is having stamina. Grit is sticking with your future, day in, day out, not just for the week, not just for the month, but for years." By embracing a growth mindset, we can approach challenges and setbacks as opportunities for growth and learning, rather than feeling defeated by them.

Another technique that can help us navigate difficult situations with confidence is to develop a strong sense of self-awareness. Chinese author, poet, and thinker, Laozi, once said, "He who knows others is wise; he who knows himself is enlightened." By developing a strong sense of self-awareness, we can understand our own strengths and weaknesses, allowing us to navigate difficult situations with a sense of self-assurance and purpose.

Here are some practical examples of how to navigate difficult situations with confidence:

1. When facing a difficult work task or project, focus on what you can control. Navigating difficult situations with confidence can be a challenging task, but it is an essential skill to possess in order to be successful in both personal and professional life. Confidence is the foundation of resilience, and it allows us to take control of our thoughts and emotions, even in the face of adversity. As the ancient Chinese philosopher Lao Tzu once said, "When you are content to be simply yourself and don't compare or compete, everyone will respect you."

2. One way to develop confidence in navigating difficult situations is to practice mindfulness. Being present in the moment allows us to focus on the task at hand, rather than getting caught up in worry and fear. Chinese author and mindfulness expert, Echart Tolle, states, "Realize deeply that the present moment is all you have. Make the NOW the primary focus of your life." By focusing on the present moment, we are better able to handle difficult situations with a clear mind and a sense of purpose.

3. Another way to navigate difficult situations with confidence is to develop a growth mindset. Chinese author and motivational speaker, Robin Sharma, states, "The only limit to our realization of tomorrow will be our doubts of today." By embracing challenges and viewing them as opportunities for growth, we are better able to approach difficult situations with a sense of optimism and determination.

4. Practical life examples of navigating difficult situations with confidence include:

5. Public speaking: To overcome the fear of public speaking, practice mindfulness by focusing on the present moment and the message you want to convey. Take deep breaths and visualize a successful outcome.
6. Job Interviews: To navigate a difficult job interview with confidence, research the company and the position beforehand, and prepare answers to potential questions. Practice mindfulness by staying present in the moment and focusing on your strengths and qualifications.
7. Conflict Resolution: To navigate a difficult conflict with confidence, practice active listening and try to understand the other person's perspective. Take a step back and focus on finding a solution that benefits both parties. As the Chinese philosopher Lao Tzu once said, "He who conquers others is strong, but he who conquers himself is mighty." By understanding and managing our own emotions, we are better equipped to understand and manage the emotions of others.
8. One practical example of this is in the workplace. When dealing with a difficult colleague or boss, it can be easy to become defensive and react emotionally. Instead, try to approach the situation with a calm and open mind. Listen actively to their concerns and try to understand where they are coming from. By doing so, you may be able to find common ground and work towards a solution that benefits both parties.
9. Another example is in personal relationships. When dealing with a difficult family member or friend, it can be easy to become upset and argue. Instead, try to approach the situation with empathy and understanding. Listen to their perspective and try to understand where they are coming from. By doing so, you may be able to find common ground and work towards a solution that benefits both parties.
10. In any difficult situation, it's important to remember that "The best way out is always through" as Robert Frost put it. Confronting and resolving conflicts may be hard, but avoiding them will only prolong the problem and make it worse in the long run.
11. Additionally, having a supportive network of friends and family can help in navigating difficult situations. As the Chinese author and poet Li Bai wrote, "A real friend is one who walks in when the rest of the world walks out." Surround yourself with people who will support and guide you through difficult situations.
12. a mountain begins by carrying away small stones." In other words, taking care of yourself and being patient with yourself is key to building the confidence and resilience needed to handle difficult situations. Self-compassion also allows you to be more understanding and compassionate towards others, which can go a long way in resolving conflicts.
13. To put this into practice, make sure to take breaks when needed, practice mindfulness and self-care activities such as exercise, meditation, or journaling. Also, try to reframe negative thoughts about yourself and the situation into more positive and compassionate ones. For example,

instead of beating yourself up for not handling a situation perfectly, remind yourself that it is normal to make mistakes and that you can learn from them.

In conclusion, navigating difficult situations with confidence is a skill that can be developed and honed through practice. It requires active listening, understanding different perspectives, and self-compassion. By following these principles, you will become more resilient in handling conflicts and challenges, and ultimately be able to find better solutions for all parties involved.

Fostering a Growth Mindset for Resilience Building.

Fostering a growth mindset is a key component in building resilience. A growth mindset is the belief that one's abilities and intelligence can be developed through effort, learning and perseverance. In contrast, a fixed mindset is the belief that one's abilities and intelligence are set in stone and cannot be changed. According to Chinese author and keynote speaker, Dr. Hongbin Song, "A fixed mindset limits our potential, while a growth mindset allows us to reach our full potential."

One of the key ways to foster a growth mindset is to embrace challenges and setbacks as opportunities for growth and learning. Chinese author and motivational speaker, Lousie Li, states "Challenges and setbacks are not obstacles, but opportunities for growth." This means that rather than shying away from difficult tasks or situations, we should approach them with a sense of curiosity and willingness to learn.

Another important aspect of fostering a growth mindset is to focus on the process rather than the outcome. Chinese author and entrepreneur, John Li, explains "Success is not about winning, but about learning and growing." This means that rather than becoming fixated on achieving a specific outcome, we should focus on the effort and progress we make along the way.

One practical way to foster a growth mindset is to actively seek out new challenges and experiences. This could mean taking on a new role or responsibility at work, learning a new skill or hobby, or trying a new activity. By stepping out of our comfort zones and exposing ourselves to new challenges, we can develop a sense of confidence and self-efficacy.

Another practical way to foster a growth mindset is to surround ourselves with people who have a growth mindset. This could mean seeking out mentors or coaches who can provide guidance and support, or connecting with a community of like-minded individuals who are also committed to personal growth and development.

Furthermore, practicing mindfulness and self-reflection can also foster a growth mindset. Chinese author and meditation teacher, Master Mingtong Gu, states "Mindfulness is about seeing things as they are , not as we wish them to be. It is about being present in the moment and observing our thoughts and emotions without judgment. When we practice mindfulness, we are able to step back and see our thoughts and emotions objectively, rather than getting caught up in them. This allows us to challenge limiting beliefs and develop a more positive outlook on life."

By regularly taking time to check in with ourselves and observe our thoughts and emotions, we can begin to notice patterns and areas where we tend to have a fixed mindset. Through self-reflection, we can start to challenge these limiting beliefs and develop a more growth-oriented mindset.

One practical example of fostering a growth mindset through mindfulness and self-reflection is by setting aside time each day to journal. During this time, we can reflect on our thoughts, emotions, and experiences from the day. By identifying patterns of fixed mindset thinking, we can begin to challenge and replace them with more growth-oriented thoughts.

Another practical example is through the practice of meditation. By focusing on the present moment and observing our thoughts without judgment, we can learn to let go of negative thoughts and emotions that limit our potential. Additionally, the practice of gratitude can also foster a growth mindset by shifting our focus from our shortcomings to our strengths and blessings.

Chinese author, teacher and speaker, Lao Tzu, once said "Nature does not hurry, yet everything is accomplished." This quote reminds us that true growth and progress takes time and patience. Instead of expecting immediate results, we can learn to embrace the process and trust in our ability to grow and improve over time.

One practical example of embracing the process and trusting in our ability to grow is by setting small, achievable goals for ourselves. By breaking down larger goals into smaller, manageable steps, we can see progress and improvement, which can lead to increased self-confidence and motivation to keep going. Another example is by surrounding ourselves with positive and supportive people, who are also growth-minded, and can encourage and inspire us to continue to push ourselves and challenge our limitations.

Another practical way to foster a growth mindset is through learning and taking on new challenges. Chinese author and entrepreneur, Jack Ma, states, "If you want to be successful, you have to be willing to learn and be willing to be taught." By challenging ourselves to learn new skills or take on new projects, we can push past our comfort zones and develop a stronger sense of self-efficacy.

Finally, it is important to be open to feedback and to see mistakes and failures as opportunities for growth and learning. Chinese author and businessman, Li Ka-shing, says "Successful people are not afraid of failure, but understand that it is necessary for growth." By viewing failure as an opportunity for growth, we can build resilience and develop a strong sense of self-awareness, which can lead to long-term success.

In conclusion, fostering a growth mindset is essential for building resilience and achieving success. By embracing the process of growth, being open to learning and taking on new challenges, and viewing mistakes and failures as opportunities for growth, we can develop a strong sense of self-efficacy and self-awareness that can lead to long-term success. Practicing mindfulness and self-reflection, setting small goals, surrounding ourselves with positive and supportive people, and being open to feedback are practical ways we can foster a growth mindset and build resilience in our personal and professional lives.

Chapter Ten: Building a Support System: Finding Your Tribe

The Power of Parenting Communities

As a personal development expert, I want to share with you an uncommon yet truly powerful concept: the power of parenting communities.

First, let's define what we mean by parenting communities. These are groups of parents who come together to support each other in their parenting journey. They can take many forms, such as in-person support groups, online forums, or even virtual communities on social media. The key element is that they provide a safe and supportive space for parents to share their struggles, triumphs, and learn from each other.

But why are parenting communities so powerful? One modern Spanish author, Isabel Allende, once said, "We do not inherit the earth from our ancestors, we borrow it from our children." This quote highlights the enormous responsibility we have as parents to not only raise our children to be the best versions of themselves, but also to contribute positively to the world they will inherit. Parenting communities provide a way for us to connect with other parents who share this same sense of responsibility and accountability.

Another modern Indian author, Jhumpa Lahiri, said "The role of a parent is to offer unconditional love, to provide a safe, nurturing environment, and to impart values that will serve the child throughout his or her life." Parenting communities can provide the support and guidance we need to fulfill this role to the best of our ability. In these communities, we can share our own experiences, ask for advice, and learn from the experiences of other parents.

But enough about the theoretical benefits, let's talk about the practical examples of how parenting communities can have a positive impact on our lives.

1. Emotional Support: Being a parent can be incredibly isolating and emotionally taxing. Parenting communities provide a safe space for us to share our struggles, and to receive emotional support and validation from other parents who understand what we're going through.

2. Access to Resources: Parenting communities can serve as a wealth of information and resources. Whether it's recommendations for child development experts, tips for managing behavior issues, or As a personal development expert, I want to share with you an uncommon yet truly powerful concept: the power of parenting communities.

3. First, let's define what we mean by parenting communities. These are groups of parents who come together to support each other in their parenting journey. They can take many forms, such as in-person support groups, online forums, or even virtual communities on social media. The key element is that they provide a safe and supportive space for parents to share their struggles, triumphs, and learn from each other.

4. But why are parenting communities so powerful? One modern Spanish author, Isabel Allende, once said, "We do not inherit the earth from our ancestors, we borrow it from our children." This quote highlights the enormous responsibility we have as parents to not only raise our children to be the best versions of themselves, but also to contribute positively to the world they will inherit. Parenting communities provide a way for us to connect with other parents who share this same sense of responsibility and accountability.

5. Another modern Indian author, Jhumpa Lahiri, said "The role of a parent is to offer unconditional love, to provide a safe, nurturing environment, and to impart values that will serve the child throughout his or her life." Parenting communities can provide the support and guidance we need to fulfill this role to the best of our ability. In these communities, we can share our own experiences, ask for advice, and learn from the experiences of other parents.

6. But enough about the theoretical benefits, let's talk about the practical examples of how parenting communities can have a positive impact on our lives.

7. Emotional Support: Being a parent can be incredibly isolating and emotionally taxing. Parenting communities provide a safe space for us to share our struggles, and to receive emotional support and validation from other parents who understand what we're going through.

8. Access to Resources: Parenting communities can serve as a wealth of information and resources. Whether it's recommendations for child development experts, tips for managing behavior issues, or a parenting community, individuals can share the joys and challenges of raising children and offer emotional support to one another. Additionally, parenting communities can provide an opportunity to learn from other parents who have different parenting styles and perspectives, which can help parents to broaden their own perspectives and develop new parenting strategies.

9. Practical examples:

10. A local parent-teacher association (PTA) that organizes monthly meetings for parents to discuss school-related issues and share parenting tips.

11. A parenting support group that meets weekly at a community center to discuss various child-rearing topics and offer emotional support to one another.

12. A Facebook group for parents in a specific neighborhood or city, where members can share information about local events, resources, and parenting advice.

13. A WhatsApp group for new parents in a hospital maternity ward, where members can ask questions and share tips on baby care and parenting.

14. In addition to social support, parenting communities can also help parents to gain access to resources that they may not have otherwise known about. This is particularly important for low-income families or families living in remote areas, who may have limited access to

resources and services. Indian author, Malala Yousafzai, said, "One child, one teacher, one book, one pen can change the world." By connecting with other parents in a parenting community, individuals can learn about resources and services that can help them to improve their parenting skills and provide a better life for their children.

Practical examples:

1. A parenting community for low-income families that provides access to resources such as food banks, counseling services, and educational programs for children. This type of community can also provide support for parents in navigating complex systems such as the welfare system and public education.
2. A parenting community for single mothers that offers mentorship and support for navigating the challenges of raising children on one's own. This community can also provide a safe space for single mothers to share their experiences and provide emotional support for one another.
3. A parenting community for immigrant families that provides resources and support for navigating the unique challenges of raising children in a new culture. This community can also serve as a bridge between the parents' home culture and their new community, helping to preserve cultural identity and tradition while also promoting integration and belonging.
4. A parenting community for grandparents raising grandchildren that provides support, resources and counseling services specifically tailored to the unique challenges and responsibilities of grandparent caregivers. This community can also serve as an advocate for grandparents in navigating legal and financial issues related to raising grandchildren.
5. In conclusion, parenting communities are powerful resources that can provide access to information, resources, and social support for parents. The power of parenting communities is reflected in the words of Indian author, Jiddu Krishnamurti, "It is the function of education to help you, not to interfere. It is the function of education to help you, not to force you to conform to a pattern. It is the function of education to help you to become a light to yourself." And that's what parenting communities do; they empower parents to become their own best resource and support system for their children.

Building a Support System: The Importance of Finding Your Tribe

Building a support system is essential for personal growth and development. One of the most powerful ways to do this is by finding your tribe. A tribe is a group of people who share similar values, goals, and interests. They understand you and support you in your journey. They are the people who will be there for you when you need them, who will celebrate your successes, and who will help you through your struggles.

As the famous Spanish author, Paulo Coelho, once said, "When you find your tribe, you find yourself." This is because your tribe is made up of individuals who understand you on a deep level and who will help you to become the best version of yourself. They are the people who will challenge you to grow and who will hold you accountable for your actions.

Similarly, the Russian writer, Fyodor Dostoevsky, once said, "The greatest happiness is to know the source of unhappiness." Your tribe will help you to understand the source of your unhappiness and will work with you to overcome it. They will be there to support you through the difficult times and will help you to see things from a different perspective.

As Indian author, Jhumpa Lahiri, once said, "There's a sense of belonging when you're with your tribe." Your tribe will provide you with a sense of belonging and community that is essential for personal growth and development. They are the people who will accept you for who you are and who will love you unconditionally.

In practical life examples, building a support system through finding your tribe can manifest in many ways. For example, a person who is passionate about fitness and health may find their tribe at a local gym or fitness group. They will form connections with people who share their interest in health and wellness and who will support and motivate them in their fitness journey. Another example is for an individual who is an aspiring entrepreneur, they may find their tribe in a networking group or startup community where they can find like-minded individuals who are also working towards building their own business. This tribe can provide support and guidance in the form of mentorship, resources, and networking opportunities. As Spanish author Paulo Coelho said, "When you want something, all the universe conspires in helping you to achieve it." Finding a tribe of individuals who are working towards similar goals can help to align the universe in your favor and increase your chances of success.

Another example is for someone who is working towards personal growth and self-improvement. They may find their tribe in a therapy group or self-help community where they can connect with others who are also working towards bettering themselves. As Russian author Fyodor Dostoevsky said, "The man who does not value himself, cannot value anything or anyone." Having a tribe of individuals who understand and support your journey of self-discovery can be invaluable in helping you to build self-worth and self-esteem.

Lastly, for someone who is struggling with mental health issues, their tribe may be found in a support group or therapy group where they can connect with others who are going through similar experiences. As Indian author Jiddu Krishnamurti said, "It is no measure of health to be well adjusted to a profoundly sick society." Having a tribe of individuals who understand and support your struggles can be incredibly healing and empowering.

In conclusion, building a support system or finding your tribe is essential for personal growth and success. Whether it be in the form of a networking group, therapy group, or self-help community, having individuals who understand and support your journey can make all the difference. Remember, as the famous quote goes, "No man is an island." We all need support and connection in our lives, so don't be afraid to reach out and find your tribe.

Navigating the Parenting Journey: Finding Others Who Understand

Navigating the parenting journey can be one of the most challenging and rewarding experiences of a person's life. It can also be a lonely and isolating experience, especially when one feels like they are the only one going through certain struggles. However, it is important to remember that every parent, regardless of culture or background, goes through similar challenges and struggles. Finding others who understand and can relate to your experiences can be a powerful tool in navigating the parenting journey.

As the Spanish author Isabel Allende once said, "Being a mother is an attitude, not a biological relation." This quote highlights the idea that being a parent is not just about biology, but also about the mindset and attitude one brings to the role. It is important to remember that parenting is not just about blood relation, but also about the love and care one provides to a child.

Similarly, the Russian author Leo Tolstoy once said, "The two most powerful warriors are patience and time." This quote highlights the importance of being patient and taking the time to navigate the challenges of parenting. It is important to remember that there are no shortcuts or easy solutions to the challenges of parenting, and that it takes time, patience, and perseverance to navigate the journey.

The Indian author Jiddu Krishnamurti also said, "It is no measure of health to be well adjusted to a profoundly sick society." This quote highlights the importance of being aware of the societal expectations and pressures placed on parents and not allowing them to negatively affect one's own personal growth and development as a parent. It is important to remember to question societal norms and expectations and to strive for personal growth and development, rather than conforming to societal pressures.

In India, it is believed that "the bond between a mother and her child is the purest and most selfless form of love" (Sadhguru, Indian spiritual leader). Yet, parenting is not always a smooth journey, and it can be challenging to find others who truly understand and relate to the struggles and joys of being a parent.

In practical life examples, one way to find others who understand is to join a parenting group or support group. These groups provide a safe and non-judgmental space for parents to share their experiences and offer support and advice to one another. Another way is to find a mentor or role model who has been through similar experiences and can offer guidance and support. "In the end, it's not the years in your life that count. It's the life in your years," said Abraham Lincoln, and this is especially true when it comes to parenting. Having a mentor or role model who has been through the ups and downs of parenting can be invaluable in helping you navigate the journey.

One practical way to find a mentor is through parenting groups or support groups. These groups provide a safe and supportive space for parents to share their experiences, ask for advice, and connect with others who understand what they are going through. Joining a group like this can be a great way to find a mentor or role model who can offer guidance and support.

Another way to find a mentor is through online parenting communities. These communities are a great resource for finding other parents who understand what you're going through. They can offer advice and support, as well as connect you with other parents who have been through similar experiences.

"When it comes to parenting, there is no such thing as a perfect parent, only different kinds of imperfect ones," said Spanish author Isabel Allende. It's important to remember that no one is a perfect parent, and seeking out the guidance and support of others can help us to become the best parents we can be.

Another way to find a mentor is through parenting classes or workshops. Many communities offer parenting classes or workshops that can provide parents with a wealth of information and resources. They can also be a great way to connect with other parents who are going through similar experiences.

"Parenting is the most difficult and the most rewarding of all human experiences," said Russian author Leo Tolstoy. While parenting can be difficult, it can also be incredibly rewarding. Finding others who understand what you're going through can make the journey a little easier.

One of the most difficult aspects of the parenting journey is navigating the isolation that can come with the responsibility of raising a child. As Spanish author Isabel Allende writes, "To be a mother is to be a warrior, to be a warrior is to be a savior, to be a savior is to be a saint, to be a saint is to be a martyr, and to be a martyr is to be a mother." Being a parent often means sacrificing personal needs and desires for the well-being of one's child, and this can lead to feelings of loneliness and disconnection.

One practical way to combat this isolation is to seek out parenting support groups. These groups provide a safe space for parents to share their experiences and connect with others who understand the unique challenges and rewards of parenting. In these groups, parents can find support, validation, and a sense of community.

Another way to navigate the parenting journey is to find a mentor or role model who has been through the same experiences. Russian author Leo Tolstoy said, "The two most powerful warriors are patience and time." Finding someone who has successfully navigated the ups and downs of parenthood can provide valuable guidance and wisdom. This person can also serve as a reminder that the challenges of parenting are temporary and that there is light at the end of the tunnel.

In addition to seeking out support and guidance, it is also important to practice self-care and self-compassion. As a parent, it is easy to become consumed by the responsibilities of raising a child and to lose sight of one's own needs and well-being. Practicing self compassion is crucial in navigating the parenting journey. As the modern Spanish author, Pilar Jericó, writes, "Being a good parent means loving yourself, taking care of yourself, and not losing yourself in the process." The journey of parenting can be challenging and overwhelming at times, and it is important to remember to take care of oneself in order to be able to fully show up for one's children.

One practical way to practice self-compassion is through setting boundaries. As the Russian author, Leo Tolstoy, states, "The two most powerful warriors are patience and time." It can be easy to get caught up in the day-to-day tasks and responsibilities of parenting, but it is important to set aside time for oneself in order to recharge and maintain balance. This can be as simple as taking a few minutes each day for a quiet moment of reflection or dedicating a specific time each week for a self-care activity.

Another practical way to practice self-compassion is by seeking out a support system. As the Indian author, Jiddu Krishnamurti, writes, "It is no measure of health to be well-adjusted to a profoundly sick society." Finding other parents who understand the challenges and joys of the parenting journey can provide a sense of validation and support. This can be done through joining a local parenting group, connecting with other parents online, or even just having regular coffee dates with friends who are also navigating the journey of parenting.

Additionally, practicing mindfulness can help in navigating the parenting journey. As the author, Thich Nhat Hanh, writes, "The most precious gift we can offer anyone is our attention." Being present and fully engaged in the moment with one's children can foster deeper connections and understanding. Practicing mindfulness can be done through simple exercises such as deep breathing or a body scan, or even just taking a few minutes each day to focus on the present moment.

Lastly, Navigating the parenting journey can be a difficult and isolating experience, but finding others who understand can make a world of difference.

As the Spanish author Isabel Allende once said, "You can't change the past, but you can ruin the present by worrying about the future." As parents, it can be easy to get caught up in regrets about the past or worries about the future, but it's important to focus on the present moment and find others who understand the struggles and joys of parenting.

In the words of Russian author Leo Tolstoy, "The two most powerful warriors are patience and time." Parenting requires a great deal of patience and the ability to take things one day at a time. Connecting with other parents who have gone through similar struggles can help us find the patience and time we need to navigate the parenting journey.

As Indian author Jhumpa Lahiri once said, "The only way to endure the journey was to think of it as a story." The parenting journey is a story, a story that is not just about the child but also about the parent. Sharing our stories with others who understand can help us find meaning in the journey and make it more bearable.

1. Joining a parenting support group can be a great way to connect with others who understand the struggles and joys of parenting. These groups provide a safe and supportive space to share your experiences and gain insight and advice from others who are going through similar experiences.
2. Finding a mentor or role model who has been through the parenting journey can provide valuable guidance and support. These individuals can offer practical advice and emotional support, as well as help you navigate the many challenges of parenting.
3. Building a network of friends and family who are also parents can be a great way to find support and understanding. These individuals can provide emotional support, practical help, and a sense of community as you navigate the parenting journey.

The Benefits of Joining a Support Group: Building Connections and Finding Solutions

I can attest to the many benefits of joining a support group. One of the most significant benefits is the ability to build connections and find solutions as a lone wolf. This may seem hard to believe, but it is a truth that has been echoed by many modern authors.

Spanish author Paulo Coelho once said, "When you are alone, you are not really alone. You have your own company." Similarly, Russian author Leo Tolstoy stated, "The greatest happiness is to vanquish your enemies, to chase them before you, to rob them of their wealth, to see those dear to them bathed in tears, to clasp to your bosom their wives and daughters." These quotes highlight the importance of connection and community in our lives.

Joining a support group allows us to connect with others who have similar experiences and struggles. This connection can provide a sense of belonging and validation that is hard to find when going through difficult times alone. Indian author Jiddu Krishnamurti said, "It is no measure of health to be well adjusted to a profoundly sick society." Joining a support group allows us to step outside of a society that may not understand or support our struggles and find validation and understanding among a group of like-minded individuals.

In addition to building connections, support groups also provide a space for finding solutions. As a lone wolf, it can be easy to get stuck in a cycle of negative thoughts and behaviors. However, in a support group, we are able to bounce ideas and solutions off of one another, leading to a more diverse range of perspectives and a greater chance of finding a solution that works for us.

One practical example of the benefits of joining a support group is in the case of addiction recovery. Joining a support group such as Alcoholics Anonymous or Narcotics Anonymous allows individuals struggling with addiction to connect with others who understand their struggles and provide a sense of community and validation. The support and accountability that comes from being part of a group can be crucial in maintaining sobriety. As the famous

Spanish author, Gabriel Garcia Marquez said, "Alone, we can do so little; together we can do so much."

Another practical example of the benefits of joining a support group is for individuals dealing with mental health issues such as anxiety or depression. Joining a support group allows individuals to connect with others who are going through similar experiences, providing a sense of understanding and validation. The group can also provide a sense of hope, as members share their own stories of how they have been able to cope and improve their mental health. Indian author Jiddu Krishnamurti said, "The more you understand yourself, the more clarity there is. Self-knowledge has no end."

In the case of individuals dealing with a chronic illness such as cancer or multiple sclerosis, joining a support group can provide a sense of community and understanding. The group can provide a space for individuals to share their experiences and provide emotional support for one another. It can also serve as a source of information and resources for managing the illness. Russian author Leo Tolstoy said, "The strongest of all warriors are these two — Time and Patience."

Finally, for individuals who have experienced a significant loss such as the death of a loved one or a divorce, joining a support group can provide a sense of community and validation. The group can provide a space for individuals to grieve and process their emotions, as well as offer practical advice and resources for moving forward. As the famous Spanish author, Gabriel Garcia Marquez said , "Solitude is not the same as loneliness." Joining a support group can help individuals find solace in the company of others who understand their struggles, rather than feeling isolated in their grief.

Support groups can also be beneficial for individuals facing mental health challenges, such as anxiety or depression. In these groups, individuals can learn coping strategies and find support in others who understand the struggles of living with mental illness. As the famous Russian author, Leo Tolstoy said, "We can know only that we know nothing. And that is the highest degree of human wisdom." By joining a support group, individuals can learn from the experiences of others and gain a deeper understanding of themselves and their struggles.

For those facing addiction or substance abuse, support groups can provide a sense of accountability and a sense of purpose. Individuals can learn from the experiences of others who have overcome similar struggles, and find strength in the collective journey towards recovery. As the famous Indian author and spiritual leader, Jiddu Krishnamurti said, "It is no measure of health to be well adjusted to a profoundly sick society." Joining a support group can help individuals find a sense of healing and well-being amidst difficult circumstances.

In practical life examples,

1. A person who has recently lost their spouse can benefit from joining a support group for widows and widowers. They can find comfort in the company of others who understand

the unique challenges of losing a partner, and gain practical advice on how to navigate life without their loved one.

2. An individual struggling with anxiety can also benefit from joining a support group. The group can provide a space for individuals to share their experiences and learn from others who have been through similar struggles. The sense of belonging and connection that comes from being in a support group can also help to reduce feelings of isolation and loneliness, which can exacerbate anxiety symptoms. As the Russian author, Fyodor Dostoevsky stated, "The greatest happiness is to know the source of unhappiness." Joining a support group can provide individuals with the tools and resources to understand and manage their anxiety.

3. For individuals dealing with addiction, support groups such as Alcoholics Anonymous and Narcotics Anonymous can be a lifeline. The group provides a safe and confidential space for individuals to share their struggles and receive support and guidance from others who have been through similar experiences. The group can also provide accountability and a sense of community, which can be crucial in maintaining sobriety. As the Indian author, Jiddu Krishnamurti, said "It is no measure of health to be well-adjusted to a profoundly sick society." Joining a support group can provide individuals with the tools and resources to navigate a society that often stigmatizes addiction and find a path to recovery.

4. In addition, for individuals dealing with chronic illness, support groups can provide a sense of community and validation. The group can provide a space for individuals to share their experiences and learn from others who have been through similar struggles. The sense of belonging and connection that comes from being in a support group can also help to reduce feelings of isolation and loneliness, which can exacerbate symptoms of chronic illness. As the Indian author, Jiddu Krishnamurti, said "It is no measure of health to be well adjusted to a profoundly sick society." Joining a support group can help individuals dealing with chronic illness to not only cope with their physical symptoms, but also to gain a sense of empowerment and control over their situation.

5. Practical examples of the benefits of joining a support group include:

6. A support group for individuals dealing with addiction can provide a safe and confidential space for members to share their struggles, provide accountability, and offer practical advice for maintaining sobriety.

7. A support group for individuals dealing with mental health issues such as depression or anxiety can provide a sense of validation and understanding for members, as well as offer practical coping strategies and resources for managing symptoms.

8. A support group for individuals dealing with chronic pain can provide a sense of community and validation, as well as offer practical advice and resources for managing pain, such as physical therapy and alternative treatments.
9. A support group for caregivers of loved ones with a serious illness can provide a sense of community and validation, as well as offer practical advice and resources for managing the emotional and physical demands of caregiving.

Overall, joining a support group can provide individuals with a sense of community and validation, as well as offer practical advice and resources for addressing the challenges they are facing. As the Russian author, Leo Tolstoy, said "The only thing necessary for the triumph of evil is for good men to do nothing." Joining a support group can be a powerful step towards finding solutions and building connections, rather than feeling alone and helpless.

Chapter Eleven: Embracing Failure: Learning from Mistakes

Understanding the Role of Failure in Learning and Growth

I believe that failure plays a crucial role in learning and growth. The concept of failure is often associated with negative connotations, such as defeat, disappointment, and inadequacy. However, failure should be viewed as a valuable opportunity for growth and learning.

"Every mistake is an opportunity to learn" says Spanish author Paulo Coelho. Failure is an inevitable part of life and an essential component of the learning process. It allows us to identify our weaknesses, learn from our mistakes, and make necessary adjustments to improve our performance. Failure is not the opposite of success, but rather an integral part of it.

Being a lone wolf and working independently can be both challenging and rewarding. It can be hard to find motivation and support when working alone, and it can be even harder to handle failure. However, as a lone wolf, it is important to understand that failure is not a reflection of your abilities or worth as a person. It is simply an opportunity to learn and grow.

"In order to succeed, your desire for success should be greater than your fear of failure" says Russian author Bill Cosby. It is important to remember that failure is not the end of the road, but rather a stepping stone towards success. Instead of dwelling on failure, focus on the lessons that can be learned from it and take action to apply those lessons in the future.

In practical life examples, failure can be seen in various aspects such as;

1. In a professional setting, a failed project can teach valuable lessons on time management, communication, and team dynamics.
2. In a personal relationship, a failed relationship can teach valuable lessons on communication, trust, and compromise.
3. In fitness, a failed workout can teach valuable lessons on proper form, technique, and recovery.
4. In academics, a failed exam can teach valuable lessons on study habits, time management, and understanding the material.

In conclusion, as a lone wolf, it is essential to understand the role of failure in learning and growth. Failure should be seen as a natural part of the learning process and not as a setback or a sign of weakness. As the Spanish author and philosopher, Miguel de Unamuno, once said, "I cannot believe in a God who wants to be praised all the time." Similarly, we should not be afraid of failure, but instead embrace it as an opportunity to learn and grow.

One practical example of this understanding is in the world of entrepreneurship. Many successful entrepreneurs have failed multiple times before finding success. For example, the founder of Airbnb, Brian Chesky, had to face several failures before finally achieving success. He learned from each failure and was able to adapt and improve his business model, ultimately leading to the success of Airbnb.

Another practical example is in the field of sports. Athletes who have achieved great success often attribute their success to the failures they have faced along the way. The Russian gymnast, Svetlana Khorkina, once said, "I have failed more than 9,000 times in my career. Every failure taught me something new." She understood that failure was a necessary part of the learning process and used it to improve her performance.

In the personal development world, failure is also an essential aspect of growth. Sometimes, we may have to face difficult situations and may not come out successful, but it is through these failures that we learn important life lessons and become stronger individuals.

Lastly, in the field of scientific research, failure is a common occurrence. Scientists often have to conduct many experiments before finding the right solution or answer. They understand that failure is a natural part of the research process and use it as a learning opportunity to improve their methods and findings.

In conclusion, failure should not be seen as a negative thing, but instead as an opportunity to learn and grow. As the Russian author and poet, Fy odor Dostoevsky once said, "The degree of civilization in a society can be judged by entering its prisons." Similarly, one's personal growth and development can be measured by their ability to accept and learn from their failures.

In the words of Spanish author, Paulo Coelho, "I think you can have 10,000 explanations for failure, but no good explanation for success." This highlights the fact that failure is a natural and integral part of life, and it is important to understand that success cannot be fully appreciated without experiencing failure.

One practical example of this is the process of learning a new skill or trade. Often times, beginners will encounter challenges and make mistakes, but it is through these failures that they are able to improve and master their craft. Similarly, in the field of entrepreneurship, successful business owners have likely faced numerous failures before achieving success.

Another example can be seen in personal relationships. It is through the experiences of failed relationships that individuals are able to learn and grow, ultimately leading them to healthier and more fulfilling connections in the future.

Lastly, in the professional world, failure in a project or task can provide valuable lessons for future endeavors and lead to improved teamwork and problem-solving skills.

In short, failure should not be feared, but embraced as a necessary step in the journey of learning and growth. As the Russian author, Leo Tolstoy said, "The two most powerful warriors are patience and time." By understanding the role of failure and being patient, one can ultimately achieve success and reach their full potential.

Overcoming the Fear of Failure: Strategies for Parents

Overcoming the fear of failure is a daunting task for many individuals, but it can be especially challenging for parents who are often the lone wolf in their households. The fear of failure can hold parents back from pursuing their goals and can prevent them from being the best version of themselves for their children. However, with the right strategies and mindset, parents can overcome this fear and become the role models their children need.

One of the first steps in overcoming the fear of failure is to understand that failure is an inevitable part of life. As the Spanish author Paulo Coelho said, "When you want something, all the universe conspires in helping you to achieve it." Failure is not a setback, but rather an opportunity to learn and grow. It is essential to embrace failure and use it as a tool for personal development.

Another strategy for overcoming the fear of failure is to focus on the present. Russian author Leo Tolstoy said, "The two most powerful warriors are patience and time." It's easy to get caught up in the future and worry about what could go wrong, but by focusing on the present, parents can take control of their thoughts and emotions. Instead of worrying about what could go wrong, parents can take action in the present moment and make the most of their opportunities.

In addition to these strategies, parents can also use practical life examples to overcome the fear of failure. For example, parents can practice taking risks in small ways. This can be as simple as trying a new recipe or taking a different route to work. By taking small risks, parents can become more comfortable with the idea of failure and learn to deal with it in a more constructive way.

Another practical example is setting small goals for yourself. This can be as simple as reading a chapter of a book every day or going for a walk every morning. By setting small goals, parents can build their confidence and become more comfortable with the idea of failure.

Lastly, parents can also use mindfulness techniques to help them overcome the fear of failure . Mindfulness is the practice of being present and fully engaged in the current moment, without judgment. It allows individuals to observe their thoughts and emotions, rather than getting caught up in them. By practicing mindfulness, parents can learn to let go of their fears and focus on the present moment.

One way to practice mindfulness is through meditation. This can be as simple as setting aside a few minutes each day to sit quietly and focus on your breath. As you breathe in and out, try to let go of any thoughts or worries that come to mind. Instead, focus on the sensation of the breath moving in and out of your body. This can help you become more aware of your thoughts and emotions, and learn to let go of them.

Another way to practice mindfulness is through journaling. Writing down your thoughts and feelings can help you gain insight into your fears and how they affect you. You can also use journaling to track your progress as you work to overcome your fear of failure.

Additionally, parents can also use visualization techniques to overcome the fear of failure. Visualization involves creating a mental image of yourself succeeding in a particular situation. This can help you to feel more confident and positive about your abilities. For example, you can visualize yourself giving a successful presentation at work or your child getting an A on a test.

Lastly, parents can also use affirmations to help them overcome the fear of failure. Affirmations are positive statements that you repeat to yourself, in order to change your mindset. For example, "I am capable of success" or "I trust in my abilities." Repeat these affirmations to yourself daily and remind yourself of your strengths and capabilities.

In conclusion, the fear of failure is a common experience for many parents. However, with the right strategies and tools, parents can learn to overcome this fear and build their confidence. By setting clear goals, developing a growth mindset, and seeking support from others, parents can learn to view failure as an opportunity for growth and development. As Spanish author Paulo Coelho said, "There is only one thing that makes a dream impossible to achieve: the fear of failure." By recognizing and addressing this fear, parents can open themselves up to new possibilities and achieve their goals.

One practical strategy that parents can use to overcome the fear of failure is to set small, achievable goals. Instead of trying to accomplish everything at once, parents can break down their goals into smaller steps and focus on achieving them one by one. This not only helps to reduce the pressure and anxiety associated with failure but also allows parents to see their progress and celebrate their successes.

Another strategy that parents can use is to develop a growth mindset. This means shifting their focus from avoiding failure to embracing it and learning from it. As Russian author and journalist, Anastasia Novykh said, "The fear of failure is not a lack of ability but a lack of will." Parents can learn to view failure as a valuable learning experience and an opportunity to develop new skills and strategies.

A third strategy that parents can use is to seek support from others. Whether it's friends, family, or professional counselors, surrounding oneself with supportive people can help parents to feel less alone and more confident in their abilities. This can be especially important for parents who are working on their personal development as a lone wolf, as it can be difficult to achieve goals without the encouragement and support of others.

Lastly, an effective way to overcome the fear of failure is to practice mindfulness. This means being present in the moment and not getting caught up in thoughts of past failures or worrying about future ones. Practicing mindfulness can help parents to shift their focus away from their fears and on to the present moment, allowing them to take action and move forward.

One strategy for practicing mindfulness is to take a few minutes each day to focus on your breath and observe your thoughts without judgment. This can help you to become more aware of your thoughts and patterns of thinking, and can help you to let go of negative thoughts and feelings that are holding you back.

Another strategy is to engage in activities that allow you to fully immerse yourself in the present moment, such as yoga, meditation, or journaling. These activities can help you to become more aware of your thoughts and feelings, and can help you to let go of negative thoughts and feelings that are holding you back.

It is important to remember that failure is a part of life and it should not be feared but rather embraced as a valuable learning experience. As the Spanish author José Ortega y Gasset once said, "Life is a series of accidents. But to live means to go out to meet them."

Additionally, it is important to understand that failure is not an endpoint, but rather a point of departure. The Russian author, Fyodor Dostoevsky, once said, “The only thing to fear is fear itself”. It is essential to understand that failure is only temporary, and it is not the end. Failure should be viewed as an opportunity to learn and grow, and not as a defeat.

Practical examples of overcoming the fear of failure as a parent include:

1. Setting small and achievable goals that will help to build confidence and momentum. For example, if you're a parent who wants to write a book, start by writing a short story or a chapter of a book first, and then gradually work your way up to writing a full-length novel.

2. Creating a support system of friends and family who can provide encouragement and motivation. This can be especially helpful for parents who feel like they are going through the process alone.

3. Practicing mindfulness and self-compassion, which can help to reduce feelings of fear and anxiety. This can be done through meditation, yoga, or journaling, for example.

4. Learning from failure, by reflecting on what went wrong and what you can do differently next time. This can help you to see failure as a learning opportunity, rather than something to be feared.

5. "The only limit to our realization of tomorrow will be our doubts of today." - Franklin D. Roosevelt

6. "Fear is not an uncommon companion in the journey of life, but it is a burden that need not be carried alone." - Paulo Coelho

7. "The greatest mistake you can make in life is continually fearing you will make one." - Elbert Hubbard

8. "The most common way people give up their power is by thinking they don't have any." - Alice Walker
9. "The only thing we have to fear is fear itself." - Franklin D. Roosevelt
10. Practical examples of overcoming the fear of failure as a parent include:
11. Setting small and achievable goals that will help to build confidence and momentum, such as reading a book a month or learning a new skill.
12. Creating a support system of friends and family who can provide encouragement and motivation, such as joining a parent support group or reaching out to a mentor for guidance.
13. Practicing mindfulness and meditation to help manage stress and anxiety. This can involve setting aside time each day for quiet reflection, focusing on deep breathing, and using guided imagery to visualize success.
14. Challenging negative self-talk and replacing it with positive affirmations. This can involve writing down and repeating statements that remind you of your strengths and capabilities, such as "I am capable and strong," "I can handle any challenge that comes my way," and "I trust in my ability to succeed."
15. Setting realistic and achievable goals, and breaking them down into smaller, manageable steps. This can involve creating a plan of action, setting deadlines, and holding yourself accountable for progress.
16. As a parent, it can be easy to fall into the trap of constantly comparing yourself to others and feeling inadequate. However, as the Spanish author and philosopher Miguel de Unamuno once said, "Comparison is the thief of joy." Instead of comparing yourself to others, focus on your own progress and growth.
17. Another way to overcome the fear of failure is to shift your focus from the outcome to the process. As the Russian author and scientist Ivan Pavlov said, "The chief condition for the achievement of a goal is the state of mind of the person who achieves it." Instead of focusing solely on the end result, focus on the steps you are taking to achieve it and the growth you are experiencing along the way.

Teaching Kids to Embrace Failure and Learn from Mistakes

I firmly believe that teaching children to embrace failure and learn from mistakes is essential for their long-term success and happiness. This may seem counterintuitive, as we often hear the phrase "failure is not an option" and are taught to avoid mistakes at all costs. However, it is important to recognize that failure and mistakes are an inevitable part of life and can actually be valuable learning opportunities.

As the Spanish author and philosopher Miguel de Unamuno once said, "Only by risking failure can one learn how to succeed." This means that in order to truly succeed, we must be willing to take risks and accept the possibility of failure. By teaching children to embrace failure, we are giving them the tools they need to take risks, learn from their mistakes, and ultimately achieve their goals.

Similarly, the Russian author and poet Alexander Pushkin wrote, "The only way to learn wisdom is by making mistakes." This highlights the importance of recognizing that mistakes are not only unavoidable, but also necessary for personal growth and development. When children learn to view mistakes as opportunities for learning and growth, they are more likely to take risks, persevere through challenges, and ultimately achieve their goals.

In addition to these philosophical perspectives, there are practical examples of how embracing failure and learning from mistakes can benefit children. -First, children who are taught to embrace failure are more likely to take risks and try new things. This can lead to increased creativity, innovation, and problem-solving skills. -Second, children who are taught to learn from their mistakes are more resilient and better able to bounce back from failure. This can lead to increased self-esteem, confidence, and determination. -Third, children who learn to embrace failure and learn from mistakes are less likely to give up or give in to setbacks. This can lead to increased perseverance, grit, and a growth mindset. -Fourth, children who learn to embrace failure and learn from mistakes are more likely to seek out help and support when they need it. This can lead to better communication skills, improved relationships, and a greater sense of community.

One way to teach children to embrace failure and learn from mistakes is through the use of storytelling. Share stories of famous figures who failed before they succeeded, such as Thomas Edison, who famously said, “I have not failed. I've just found 10,000 ways that won't work.”

Another way is through the use of games and activities that provide opportunities for children to make mistakes and learn from them. For example, in a game of chess, children can learn that losing a game is not the end, but an opportunity to learn from their mistakes and improve for next time.

It's also important to lead by example, showing children that failure and making mistakes is a natural part of life, and that it's possible to learn and grow from these experiences. This can be done through sharing personal anecdotes of our own failures and how we learned from them.

In the words of Spanish author, Paulo Coelho, “There is only one thing that makes a dream impossible to achieve: the fear of failure.” And Russian author, Leo Tolstoy, famously stated, “The two most powerful warriors are patience and time.” By teaching children to embrace failure and learn from mistakes, we are giving them the tools they need to become powerful warriors in their own right.

In conclusion, teaching children to embrace failure and learn from mistakes is an important aspect of personal development. It allows children to take risks, be more resilient, persevere, seek help and support and develop a growth mindset. It's a valuable lesson that can be taught through storytelling, games and activities and leading by example. Let's help our children to overcome the fear of failure and build their self-confidence, grit, and determination to succeed in life.

Empowering Kids to Take Risks and Learn from Failure.

I would like to bring to light an uncommon yet true concept that many parents and educators may not fully understand: empowering kids to take risks and learn from failure. It is a common belief that protecting children from failure is the best way to ensure their success, but in reality, it is the exact opposite.

"The greatest glory in living lies not in never falling, but in rising every time we fall." - Nelson Mandela

Allowing children to take risks and make mistakes is crucial for their personal growth and development. It teaches them to be resilient and independent, and to not be afraid of failure. Failure is a natural part of life and should be viewed as a valuable learning experience rather than a negative outcome.

"The only real mistake is the one from which we learn nothing" - John Powell

It is important to teach children to view failure as an opportunity to learn and grow. This can be done by encouraging them to try new things, even if they may not succeed at first. It is also important to provide them with a safe and supportive environment where they can take risks and make mistakes without fear of judgement or punishment.

"A person who never made a mistake never tried anything new." - Albert Einstein

One practical example of empowering kids to take risks and learn from failure is by encouraging them to participate in extracurricular activities. This can be anything from sports teams to drama clubs, and allows children to try new things and push themselves out of their comfort zone. It also teaches them the importance of perseverance and the value of hard work.

Another example is allowing children to make small decisions for themselves, such as what to wear or what to eat for breakfast. This helps them to develop decision-making skills and learn to take responsibility for their actions.

Encouraging children to take risks and make mistakes also means giving them the space and freedom to explore their interests and passions. This could be in the form of allowing them to pursue a hobby or extracurricular activity, or by providing opportunities for them to try new things and push themselves out of their comfort zones. "The only way to avoid mistakes is to have no new experiences" a quote from the Spanish author, Miguel de Cervantes.

One practical life example of this is allowing children to participate in sports or other physical activities. Not only does this promote physical health and fitness, but it also teaches children the importance of practice and perseverance, as well as the valuable lesson of learning from losses and mistakes. "The man who makes no mistakes does not usually make anything" a quote from the Russian author, Edward John Phelps.

Another example is encouraging children to express themselves creatively through art, music, or writing. This not only allows them to explore their imagination and individuality, but it also teaches them the importance of taking risks and trying new things in order to grow and improve. "The only way to do great work is to love what you do" a quote from the modern Spanish author, Steve Jobs.

Lastly, providing children with opportunities to travel and experience different cultures and perspectives can also be a valuable way to teach them about taking risks and learning from failure. This could include a family trip to a new city or country, or even a short camping or hiking excursion. "Travel is fatal to prejudice, bigotry, and narrow-mindedness" a quote from the modern author, Mark Twain.

In conclusion, empowering kids to take risks and learn from failure is an essential part of personal development and growth.

Chapter Twelve: Managing Stress and Burnout: Maintaining Balance

Understanding the Signs of Stress and Burnout

As a personal development expert, I understand that working as a "lone wolf" can be challenging, but it can also be incredibly rewarding. However, it's important to understand the signs of stress and burnout that can come with this lifestyle, and to take steps to prevent or manage them.

One of the key signs of stress and burnout as a lone wolf is a feeling of isolation. As the Spanish author, Carlos Ruiz Zafon, once said, "I am the literary equivalent of a lone wolf." This quote highlights the fact that working alone can lead to feelings of isolation and disconnection, even if you're surrounded by people.

Another sign of stress and burnout as a lone wolf is a sense of overwhelming responsibility. As Russian author, Fyodor Dostoevsky, once wrote, "The greatest and most important problems of life are all fundamentally insoluble. They can never be solved but only outgrown." This quote illustrates the idea that when we take on too much responsibility, it can become overwhelming and lead to burnout.

Another key sign of stress and burnout as a lone wolf is a loss of motivation and passion. As Russian author, Leo Tolstoy, once said, "The two most powerful warriors are patience and time." This quote highlights the idea that when we are constantly pushing ourselves, it can lead to burnout and a loss of passion and motivation.

So, how can you prevent or manage stress and burnout as a lone wolf? Here are four practical examples:

1. Connect with others: Make an effort to connect with other people in your field or community. Join a professional organization, attend networking events, or start a mentorship program. This will help you feel less isolated and more connected to others.

2. Prioritize self-care: As a lone wolf, it's important to take care of yourself both physically and mentally. Set aside time for exercise, meditation, or other self-care activities to help prevent burnout .

3. Set boundaries: It's easy to get caught up in work as a lone wolf, but it's important to set boundaries to ensure you have time for yourself and to prevent burnout. This can include setting specific work hours, taking regular breaks, and setting limits on the number of projects you take on at one time.

4. Find a support system: Whether it's a therapist, a coach, or a close friend, it's important to have someone you can talk to and confide in. They can provide a sounding board for your ideas and help you navigate any challenges you may be facing.

"Stress is the trash of modern life - we all generate it but if you don't dispose of it properly, it will pile up and overtake your life." - Danzae Pace

"Burnout is a state of emotional, physical, and mental exhaustion caused by excessive and prolonged stress." - Maslach

"The biggest problem for a lone wolf is that it's very hard to see the forest for the trees." - Alexander Pushkin

In conclusion, understanding the signs of stress and burnout is crucial for anyone, especially for lone wolves who may not have the support system of a team or colleagues. By connecting with others, prioritizing self-care, setting boundaries, and finding a support system, you can prevent burnout and maintain a healthy work-life balance. Remember, as the Spanish author, Eduardo Punset said, "The most important thing is to enjoy your life - to be happy - it's all that matters."

Strategies for Managing Stress and Burnout

Stress and burnout are common problems that many people face, especially those who work independently or as a "lone wolf." However, by implementing certain strategies and adopting the right mindset, it is possible to manage and overcome these challenges.

First and foremost, it is important to understand that stress and burnout are not simply physical or mental issues, but rather a combination of both. As Jordan Peterson, the renowned psychologist and author, states, "the body and the mind cannot be separated." Therefore, it is crucial to take care of both your physical and mental health to manage stress and burnout.

One effective strategy is to establish a daily routine and stick to it. This can include regular exercise, healthy eating, and setting aside time for self-care and relaxation. Additionally, finding a hobby or activity that you enjoy can be a great way to de-stress and recharge. As the famous author Mario Puzo once said, "the absence of leisure is the absence of life."

Another important strategy is to set realistic goals and priorities. This means learning to say "no" to unnecessary tasks and focusing on what is truly important. As Anne Rice, the bestselling author, puts it, "the worst thing you can do is not make a decision at all." By setting clear goals and priorities, you can avoid feeling overwhelmed and better manage your time and energy.

In addition to these strategies, it is also important to adopt a positive mindset and attitude. This means learning to accept and embrace challenges as opportunities for growth and development. As the modern Russian author, Victor Pelevin, says , "Life is a game, and the game is a battle. It is a battle not against others, but against yourself." Embracing this mindset means recognizing that stress and burnout are natural parts of the process, and that they are not necessarily negative. Instead, they can be seen as opportunities to push yourself further and develop new skills and strengths.

Another important strategy for managing stress and burnout as a lone wolf is to focus on building a strong sense of purpose and meaning in your work. This can involve setting clear goals and working towards them, as well as finding ways to connect your work to something larger than yourself. As the Norwegian author, Lars Mytting, writes, "The best way to fight stress is to find a cause that is greater than yourself." By focusing on something bigger than yourself, you can tap into a deeper sense of motivation and drive, which can help you to push through difficult times.

In addition to these strategies, it's important to set boundaries and protect your time. This means learning to say no to requests and obligations that don't align with your goals and priorities. As Anne Rice writes in "The Witching Hour" "You can't give what you haven't got." Taking care of yourself and your needs first will allow you to be more effective and efficient in your work, and less likely to burnout.

Ultimately, managing stress and burnout as a lone wolf requires a combination of practical strategies, a positive mindset, and a strong sense of purpose and meaning. By embracing the challenge, setting boundaries, and focusing on something bigger than yourself, you can overcome burnout and emerge stronger and more resilient than ever before.

The Importance of Self-Care and Self-Compassion

As a lone wolf, it can be easy to fall into the trap of thinking that self-care and self-compassion are luxuries that you can't afford. After all, you have to fend for yourself and rely on your own strength and resilience to survive. But the truth is, self-care and self-compassion are essential for the well-being of any lone wolf, and neglecting them can lead to burnout, depression, and a host of other negative consequences.

Self-care can take many forms, from physical self-care practices like getting enough sleep and exercise, to emotional self-care practices like setting boundaries and learning to say no. It's also important to make time for activities that bring you joy and fulfillment, whether that's reading, writing, drawing, or playing music. By making self-care a priority, you are investing in your own well-being, which in turn will make you more capable of facing the challenges that come with being a lone wolf.

Self-compassion is also an essential aspect of self-care. It's easy to fall into the trap of being overly critical and judgmental of yourself, especially when you're a lone wolf. But by learning to be kind and compassionate towards yourself, you can begin to break down the negative self-talk and limiting beliefs that are holding you back.

Jordan Peterson, a Canadian psychologist and author, once said, "You must take care of yourself, so that you can take care of others." This is especially true for lone wolves, who often feel a sense of responsibility to take care of others and may neglect their own self-care.

Self-care is crucial for the physical, emotional, and mental well-being of an individual. It encompasses a range of activities that aim to improve one's overall health and happiness. For lone wolves, this may include things like regular exercise, healthy eating, getting enough sleep, and practicing mindfulness.

Self-compassion, on the other hand, is about being kind and understanding towards oneself. It means acknowledging and accepting one's own flaws and weaknesses, instead of constantly criticizing and judging oneself. This can be especially difficult for lone wolves, who may be used to pushing themselves to the limit and putting others first.

Practicing self-care and self-compassion can be challenging, but it is essential for lone wolves to take these steps in order to maintain their physical, emotional, and mental well-being. Life examples from modern Russian and Norwegian authors, Jordan Peterson, Mario Puzo, Anne Rice to support this statement.

For instance, in his book "The Godfather", Mario Puzo shows how the main character, Vito Corleone, is able to maintain his power and control despite the many challenges he faces, by putting his family first and taking care of himself. Similarly, in her novel "Interview with the Vampire", Anne Rice illustrates how the main character, Louis, struggles with guilt and self-loathing, but eventually learns to accept himself and practice self-compassion.

In the same way, modern Russian and Norwegian authors have also shown how the importance of self-care and self-compassion can be applied to everyday life. For example, they illustrate how it is necessary to prioritize one's own needs, set boundaries, and practice self-compassion in order to maintain emotional balance and well-being, despite the challenges and struggles of life.

The bottom line is that self-care and self-compassion are essential for lone wolves, who often feel a sense of responsibility to take care of others. It is important to take the time to take care of oneself, both physically and emotionally, in order to be able to take care of others and live a fulfilling life.

Building Resilience: How to Bounce Back from Stress and Burnout

Being a lone wolf can be challenging, especially when it comes to building resilience in the face of stress and burnout. However, it is possible to bounce back and become stronger than ever before. Here are some practical tips and inspiration from some of the greatest minds in literature to help you on your journey.

First and foremost, it is important to understand that stress and burnout are a normal part of life. As William Shakespeare once wrote, "To be, or not to be: that is the question: Whether 'tis nobler in the mind to suffer the slings and arrows of outrageous fortune." It is important to acknowledge that these struggles are a part of the human experience, and that you are not alone in your struggles.

One of the key elements of building resilience is learning to manage your thoughts and emotions. As Agatha Christie wrote, "It is absurd to divide people into good and bad. People are either charming or tedious." By learning to control your thoughts and emotions, you can begin to see the positive in even the most challenging situations.

Another important aspect of building resilience is learning to take care of yourself. This includes both physical and emotional self-care. As Danielle Steel wrote, "The best love is the kind that awakens the soul and makes us reach for more, that plants a fire in our hearts and brings peace to our minds. And that, my friends, is what true love is all about." Make sure to prioritize your physical and emotional well-being, whether that means taking a yoga class, going for a walk, or indulging in your favorite hobby.

It's also important to remember that resilience is not about never experiencing failure or hardship, but about how you handle it. As Harold Robbins wrote, "Success is often achieved by those who don't know that failure is inevitable." Embrace your failures and learn from them. Every failure is an opportunity to learn and grow.

Another key to building resilience is to have a positive attitude, as J.K. Rowling wrote, "Happiness can be found, even in the darkest of times, if one only remembers to turn on the light." Cultivate a positive outlook and focus on the good in every situation. This will help you to bounce back more quickly when faced with stress and burnout.

Finally, it's important to remember that resilience is a journey and not a destination. As Stephen King wrote, "The most important things are the hardest to say. They are the things you get ashamed of, because words diminish them." Embrace the journey and know that it is never too late to start building resilience.

In conclusion, building resilience as a lone wolf can be challenging but it is not impossible. Remember to acknowledge the normalcy of stress and burnout, learn to manage your thoughts and emotions, take care of yourself, embrace your failures, cultivate a positive attitude and remember that resilience is a journey. Quotations from William Shakespeare, Agatha Christie, Danielle Steel, Harold Robbins, J.K Rowling and Stephen King can serve as inspiration and motivation.

Finding Balance in Your Life: Prioritizing Self-Care

When it comes to finding balance in our lives, it can be easy to focus on external factors such as work, relationships, and societal expectations. However, the key to true balance lies in the internal practice of self-care. As a "lone wolf," it can be especially important to prioritize self-care in order to maintain a healthy and fulfilling lifestyle.

One of the first steps in prioritizing self-care is understanding the importance of self-awareness. This means taking the time to understand your own needs, wants, and boundaries. It means being honest with yourself about what is truly important to you, and making the necessary adjustments in your life to align with those values. For example, if you value your mental health and well-being, it may be necessary to set boundaries with work and social obligations to make sure you have enough time for self-care activities such as meditation or therapy.

Another important aspect of self-care as a "lone wolf" is learning to rely on yourself for fulfillment and validation. As a lone wolf, you may not have a traditional support system in the form of close friends or family, but that doesn't mean you can't find fulfillment and validation within yourself. This may mean developing a daily self-care practice, such as journaling or practicing gratitude, or setting small, achievable goals for yourself and celebrating your successes.

One practical way to prioritize self-care is by scheduling in "me-time" into your daily routine. This could be as simple as taking a 15-minute break during the workday to meditate or read a book, or setting aside a specific time each week to indulge in a hobby or activity that brings you joy. It's important to note that self-care isn't just about physical activities, but also about taking care of your mental and emotional well-being.

Another way to prioritize self-care is by setting boundaries. This means learning to say no to commitments and responsibilities that don't align with your values or that drain your energy. It also means setting limits on the amount of time you spend on work or other obligations, so that you have time for yourself.

One of the best ways to prioritize self-care as a lone wolf is through mindfulness. Mindfulness is the practice of being present in the moment, and it can help you to feel more connected to yourself and the world around you. Mindfulness can be practiced through meditation, yoga, or other forms of contemplative practice.

Another practical way to prioritize self-care is by building a strong support system. This doesn't necessarily mean that you need to have a large group of friends or family members, but rather that you surround yourself with people who lift you up and who you can rely on. Whether it's joining a club or group, or simply reaching out to a friend or therapist, having someone to talk to and share your feelings with can be incredibly beneficial.

Additionally, it's important to practice self-compassion. This means treating yourself with the same kindness, concern, and understanding that you would offer to a good friend. It's important to remember that it's okay to make mistakes and that you are doing the best you can.

Finally, one of the most practical ways to prioritize self-care as a lone wolf is by setting realistic goals for yourself. This means setting goals that are achievable and that align with your values. When you set goals for yourself, make sure they are specific, measurable, and realistic.

Additionally, make sure that you are setting goals that align with your values and that are important to you.

In conclusion, self-care is important for everyone, and it's especially important for those who are lone wolves. By scheduling in "me-time," setting boundaries, practicing mindfulness, building a strong support system, practicing self-compassion, and setting realistic goals, you can prioritize self-care and find balance in your life. Remember, self-care is not selfish, it's necessary for our well-being. It's important to take care of ourselves so that we can be the best version of ourselves and take care of others.

The Role of Mindfulness in Managing Stress and Burnout

As a motivational and self-development expert, I can tell you that mindfulness is one of the most powerful tools you can use to manage stress and burnout, especially if you are a lone wolf. Mindfulness is the practice of being fully present in the moment, and it can help you to focus on the present rather than dwelling on the past or worrying about the future.

One of the key benefits of mindfulness is that it can help to reduce stress and anxiety. Stress is often caused by worrying about things that might happen in the future or dwelling on things that have happened in the past. Mindfulness helps you to focus on the present moment, which can help you to let go of those worries and anxieties.

Another benefit of mindfulness is that it can help you to manage burnout. Burnout is a state of emotional, physical, and mental exhaustion caused by prolonged stress. It can lead to feelings of cynicism, detachment, and a lack of accomplishment. Mindfulness can help you to manage your energy levels, by bringing your focus to the present and helping you to let go of the stress and anxiety that can lead to burnout.

One practical way to implement mindfulness in your life is through meditation. Meditation is a powerful tool for developing mindfulness. It can help you to focus on your breath, which can calm your mind and help you to relax. Regular meditation practice can also help you to cultivate mindfulness in your daily life.

Another practical example of mindfulness is through journaling. Journaling is a great way to process your thoughts and feelings and to reflect on your experiences. By journaling, you can gain insights into your thoughts, emotions, and behaviors , and learn how to manage them more effectively. For example, if you are feeling stressed and overwhelmed, you can write down your thoughts and feelings in your journal. This can help you to identify patterns and triggers that are causing your stress, and to develop strategies to manage them more effectively.

Another way to practice mindfulness as a lone wolf is through meditation. Meditation is a powerful tool for managing stress and burnout because it helps to quiet the mind and to focus on the present moment. This can help to reduce the impact of negative thoughts and emotions, and to increase feelings of calm and well-being. There are many different types of meditation, such as mindfulness meditation, guided meditation, and transcendental meditation. Each type has its own unique benefits, so it is important to find the one that works best for you.

Another important aspect of mindfulness is self-care. Self-care is essential for managing stress and burnout because it helps to replenish your energy and to keep you feeling balanced and grounded. Self-care can include activities such as exercise, yoga, reading, and spending time in nature. By taking time for yourself and engaging in activities that you enjoy, you can reduce your stress levels and improve your overall well-being.

One final practical example of mindfulness is through gratitude. Cultivating an attitude of gratitude can help to shift your focus away from the negative and towards the positive. By taking time to reflect on the things that you are grateful for, you can increase your feelings of contentment and happiness, and reduce feelings of stress and burnout. You can do this by writing down three things you are grateful for each day in a gratitude journal, or by sharing them with a loved one or a supportive friend.

In conclusion, mindfulness is a powerful tool for managing stress and burnout as a lone wolf. By developing a regular practice of mindfulness, you can learn to quiet the mind and focus on the present moment, gain insight into your thoughts and emotions, and develop strategies for managing them more effectively. Whether it be through journaling, meditation, self-care, or cultivating an attitude of gratitude, mindfulness can help you to reduce stress and improve your overall well-being.

How to Create a Support System for Managing Stress and Burnout.

As a lone wolf, it can be challenging to manage stress and burnout without a support system. However, it is not impossible. With a little creativity and determination, you can create a support system that works for you and helps you manage stress and burnout effectively.

One of the most important things to remember when creating a support system for stress and burnout management is that it should be tailored to your specific needs. This means that you should take into account your personality, lifestyle, and work schedule when creating your support system.

One way to create a support system for stress and burnout management is to build a network of people who can offer you emotional support. This can include friends, family members, or a therapist. They can be your sounding board for your ideas, frustrations, and concerns. They can also be a source of encouragement, motivation, and inspiration when you need it the most.

Another way to create a support system for stress and burnout management is to build a community of people who have similar interests and goals. This can include joining a club, a group, or an online community that is dedicated to a particular hobby, interest, or cause. This can be a great way to connect with like-minded individuals, share experiences and learn from one another.

To create a support system for stress and burnout management, it is also important to have a self-care routine in place. This can include things like exercise, yoga, meditation, or journaling. These activities can help you relax, de-stress, and focus on the present moment.

A practical example of building a support system for stress and burnout as a lone wolf is through developing a personal accountability system. A personal accountability system is a set of practices and routines that you put in place to ensure that you are taking care of yourself and managing your stress levels on a regular basis.

One way to create a personal accountability system is to set daily, weekly, and monthly goals for yourself that are related to self-care and stress management. For example, you might set a daily goal to exercise for 30 minutes, a weekly goal to meditate for 15 minutes, and a monthly goal to schedule a massage or other form of relaxation therapy.

Another important aspect of creating a support system for stress and burnout management is to establish a network of people who you can turn to when you need help. This might include friends, family members, or professional contacts who you can rely on to offer support, advice, or a listening ear.

One practical example of building a support network is by joining a support group or online community. There are many online communities and forums that are dedicated to helping people manage stress and burnout, and these can be a great resource for finding support and advice from others who are going through similar experiences.

Another practical example of building a support system is by developing a self-care routine that includes things like exercise, yoga, meditation, or journaling. These activities can help you relax, de-stress, and focus on the present moment.

Another practical example of building a support system for stress and burnout management is by building a habit of gratitude. This habit can be practiced by listing 3 things you are grateful for every day. This habit can help shift focus from negative thoughts to positive thoughts, which can help reduce stress and burnout.

Finally, it is important to remember that managing stress and burnout is an ongoing process, and that it is important to be patient with yourself and to continue to make adjustments as needed. With the right support system in place, you can manage stress and burnout more effectively and maintain a sense of balance and well-being in your life.

Chapter Thirteen: The Power of Visioning: Creating a Vision for Your Life

Understanding the Importance of Visioning

Being a lone wolf in today's society can be both a blessing and a curse. On one hand, you have the freedom to make your own choices, set your own goals, and chart your own course in life. On the other hand, you may feel isolated, disconnected, and unfulfilled. One key to thriving as a lone wolf is understanding the importance of visioning.

Visioning is the process of creating a clear, compelling, and compelling image of your ideal future. It is a powerful tool that can help you tap into your inner wisdom and align your actions with your deepest values and desires. By regularly engaging in visioning exercises, you can gain clarity on what you truly want, build momentum towards your goals, and create a sense of purpose and direction in your life.

One practical life example of visioning is a successful entrepreneur who started as a lone wolf in a small garage and through visioning, he was able to build a successful business empire. He began by envisioning the kind of company he wanted to create and the impact he wanted to make on the world. He then took small, consistent steps towards that vision, even in the face of obstacles and setbacks. Today, his company is one of the most well-known and respected in its industry, and he continues to use visioning to guide its growth and expansion.

Another practical life example is a lone wolf who was stuck in a dead-end job and felt unfulfilled. She began to vision of the kind of life she truly wanted, free from the constraints of a 9-5 job and with the ability to travel and explore the world. She began to research different career paths and eventually found her passion in digital marketing. She began to learn and educate herself on the necessary skills, networked with professionals in the field, and eventually landed a remote job as a digital marketer. With her newfound freedom and flexibility, she was able to travel and see the world while building a career she truly loved.

This example illustrates the power of visioning as a lone wolf. When we are able to clearly envision the life we want, we are able to set specific goals and take action towards achieving them. It requires being honest with yourself, facing your fears and limitations, and having the courage to take risks and make changes.

Another example is a lone wolf who had always dreamed of starting their own business. Despite feeling uncertain and intimidated, he began to vision and research different business ideas. He attended networking events, read books on entrepreneurship, and saved money for startup costs. Eventually, he took the leap and started his own successful business, something he never would have thought possible before.

Being a lone wolf can also mean facing rejection and setbacks along the way. But visioning allows us to see past these obstacles and stay focused on our long-term goals. It helps us to stay motivated and persevering even when faced with difficulties.

In conclusion, visioning as a lone wolf is crucial for personal and professional growth. It allows us to identify our passions and purpose, set specific goals, and take action towards achieving them. It requires honesty, courage, and persistence, but the rewards are worth it. Remember, as a lone wolf, you have the ability to shape your own future and create the life you truly want.

Setting Clear Goals and Intentions

Setting clear goals and intentions as a lone wolf is a powerful tool for achieving success in any area of life. The ability to focus on a specific outcome and take consistent action towards it is what separates those who accomplish their goals from those who simply dream about them. As a lone wolf, it's easy to get caught up in the day-to-day hustle of life and lose sight of the bigger picture. However, by setting clear goals and intentions, you can stay on track and make steady progress towards achieving your aspirations.

One of the key benefits of setting clear goals and intentions as a lone wolf is that it helps to increase your motivation and focus. When you have a specific outcome in mind, it's much easier to stay motivated and take action towards it. This is because you have a clear idea of what you want to achieve, and you know that every step you take is bringing you closer to your goal. Additionally, when you set clear goals and intentions, you have a sense of direction and purpose, which makes it easier to stay focused on what's important.

Another benefit of setting clear goals and intentions as a lone wolf is that it helps to increase your accountability. When you have a specific goal in mind, it's much easier to measure your progress and hold yourself accountable for your actions. This is because you have a clear idea of what you want to achieve, and you can use this as a benchmark to measure your progress. Additionally, when you set clear goals and intentions, you have a sense of ownership over your actions, which makes it easier to take responsibility for your results.

One practical example Setting clear goals and intentions as a lone wolf can be a challenging task, but it is not impossible. One practical example of how to accomplish this is through the use of visualization techniques. Visualization is a powerful tool that allows you to create a vivid mental picture of your desired outcome. This can be done by closing your eyes and imagining the end result as vividly as possible, including all the details and emotions associated with it.

For example, let's say you are a lone wolf looking to start your own business. You have a clear vision of what you want your business to look like, but you don't know how to get there. You can begin by visualizing yourself as the owner of a successful business, complete with a thriving customer base, a team of dedicated employees, and a steady stream of revenue. Imagine yourself in the office, surrounded by the hustle and bustle of a thriving business, and feel the excitement and satisfaction that comes with it.

In addition to visualization, setting clear goals and intentions as a lone wolf also requires taking action. This means breaking down your desired outcome into smaller, achievable steps and taking action towards them every day. For example, if your goal is to start your own business, you can begin by researching different business models, networking with other entrepreneurs, and developing a business plan. You can also set specific milestones for yourself, such as reaching a certain number of customers or generating a certain amount of revenue within a specific time frame.

Another important aspect of setting clear goals and intentions as a lone wolf is self-discipline. Self-discipline is the ability to control your thoughts, emotions, and actions in order to achieve your goals and intentions. It is the ability to push through the tough times, to stay focused and motivated, and to overcome distractions and temptations.

One practical example of self-discipline in action is the story of J.K. Rowling, the author of the Harry Potter series. J.K. Rowling was a single mother living on welfare when she began writing the first Harry Potter book. She had a clear goal and intention to become a published author and to tell the story of Harry Potter to the world. But she faced many obstacles and distractions along the way.

Despite rejection from multiple publishers, she didn't give up on her goal. Instead, she pushed through the tough times and stayed focused on her intention. She wrote in cafes and on public transportation because she couldn't afford childcare. She disciplined herself to keep writing despite the distractions and temptations that came her way.

Through her self-discipline, J.K. Rowling was able to complete the first Harry Potter book and eventually get it published. It went on to become one of the best-selling book series of all time, and J.K. Rowling became one of the most successful authors in the world.

This story demonstrates the power of self-discipline in achieving clear goals and intentions as a lone wolf. It shows that no matter how difficult the journey may be, if you have a clear goal and intention, and you are willing to push through the tough times and stay focused and motivated, you can achieve great things.

Another practical example of self-discipline in action is the story of Michael Jordan, one of the greatest basketball players of all time. Michael Jordan was known for his relentless work ethic and his ability to push himself to the limit. He was a lone wolf who set clear goals and intentions for himself, and he worked tirelessly to achieve them.

For example, when he was cut from his high school basketball team, he set a clear goal to become the best basketball player in the world. He trained tirelessly, pushing himself to be the best. He was not just a great player but also had a great work ethic and discipline. He would wake up early every morning to train, even when he didn't feel like it. He would also watch game footage and study his opponents to find ways to improve. This self-discipline and clear goal allowed him to eventually become an NBA All-Star and win multiple championships.

Another example is of a successful entrepreneur who set a clear goal to build a successful business. She knew that in order to reach her goal, she would have to sacrifice her time and energy. She was disciplined in her work habits, waking up early and working late, even when she didn't feel like it. She also made sure to set specific, measurable goals for her business and held herself accountable for reaching them. This self-discipline and clear goal allowed her to build a successful business that is now a household name.

As a lone wolf, setting clear goals and intentions is crucial for success. It gives you direction and purpose, and allows you to focus your energy on what's important. But, it is also important to remember that self-discipline is key in reaching those goals. It takes hard work, determination and sacrifice to achieve success. So, be clear in your goals and intentions, and have the self-discipline to work hard and make sacrifices to reach them.

Creating a Vision Board for Your Life

Creating a vision board for your life as a lone wolf is a powerful tool for setting and achieving your goals. It is a visual representation of your aspirations and desires, and a constant reminder of what you are working towards. But, as a lone wolf, it can be hard to stay motivated and focused on your goals when you don't have the support of others. However, with the right mindset and some practical tips, you can harness the power of the vision board to achieve your wildest dreams.

First and foremost, it's important to understand that being a lone wolf doesn't mean you are alone in your journey. Throughout history, many great leaders and thinkers were lone wolves who achieved great things. Confucius, for example, was a lone wolf who dedicated his life to studying and teaching others about morality, ethics and politics. He said, "It does not matter how slowly you go as long as you do not stop." This quote is a powerful reminder that progress and success can come at a slow pace, but as long as you keep moving forward, you will reach your destination.

Another great example is the Greek philosopher, Aristotle, who was known for his solitary ways. He said, "We are what we repeatedly do. Excellence, then, is not an act, but a habit." This quote is a reminder that success is not a one-time event, but rather a habit that you must consistently work on. The key is to stay focused on your goals and take consistent action towards achieving them.

To create a vision board as a lone wolf, you must first identify your goals and aspirations. What do you want to achieve in your life?

This may seem like a simple question, but it's important to take the time to truly reflect on what you want for yourself. It's easy to get caught up in societal expectations or the goals of others, but it's essential to focus on what truly matters to you. As ancient Greek philosopher Epictetus once said, "First say to yourself what you would be; and then do what you have to do."

Once you have a clear understanding of your goals, it's time to gather inspiration. This can come from a variety of sources such as quotes, images, or even words that resonate with you. The key is to find things that speak to your soul and align with your goals. For example, if your goal is to travel more, you may want to include images of beautiful landscapes or pictures of famous landmarks. If you're working towards financial freedom, you may want to include quotes about abundance and prosperity.

Next, it's time to start creating your vision board. This can be done physically by cutting out images and words from magazines, or digitally by creating a collage on your computer. The important thing is that it is visually pleasing and easy to look at daily.

It's also important to remember that a vision board is not a one-time activity. It's a living, breathing representation of your goals and aspirations, and should be updated as your goals and aspirations change. As the ancient Chinese philosopher Lao Tzu said, "The journey of a thousand miles begins with one step." Your vision board is the first step in that journey and should be updated as you take more steps towards your goals.

As a lone wolf, it's easy to feel like you're on your own, but it's important to remember that you have the power to shape your own life. A vision board is a powerful tool that can help you stay focused and motivated on your goals. It's a reminder of what you're working towards and the person you want to become.

Another important thing to keep in mind is to be realistic with your goals. It's easy to get carried away and want everything at once but it's important to remember that Rome wasn't built in a day. Don't be too hard on yourself and don't feel discouraged if things don't happen overnight. As ancient Greek philosopher Aristotle said, "We are what we repeatedly do. Excellence, then, is not an act, but a habit." It takes consistency, hard work, and patience to achieve your goals.

Additionally, it's important to remember that a vision board should not be limited to only materialistic goals, it should also include emotional, mental and spiritual goals. As ancient Greek philosopher Pythagoras said, "The highest realms of thought are impossible to reach without first attaining an understanding of compassion."

It's also important to remember that a vision board is not a magic wand that will make your goals come true. It's a tool to help you focus, stay motivated and remind you of your aspirations. It's important to take action towards your goals, be it small or big steps. As ancient Greek philosopher Heraclitus said, "You cannot step twice into the same river, for other waters are constantly flowing on."

In conclusion, creating a vision board as a lone wolf can be a powerful tool to help you stay focused and motivated on your goals. It's important to identify your goals and aspirations, gather inspiration, create your vision board and update it as your goals change. Remember to be realistic, consistent, and take action towards your goals. A vision board is not a magic wand but a tool to help you on your journey, as ancient philosopher Lao Tzu once said, "The journey of a thousand miles begins with one step." Take that first step towards your vision, and don't let being a lone wolf hold you back. As the ancient Greek philosopher Aristotle said, "Where your talents and the needs of the world cross, there lies your vocation." Trust in yourself and your abilities, and let your vision board be a constant reminder of the person you aspire to be and the life you desire to live. Take inspiration from the greats of ancient civilizations, who also ventured alone on their personal quests for knowledge and fulfillment, such as the famous Chinese philosopher Confucius, who once said, "The will to win, the desire to succeed, the urge to reach your full potential... these are the keys that will unlock the door to personal excellence." Creating a vision board as a lone wolf can be a powerful tool to help you stay focused and motivated on your goals. It's important to identify your goals and aspirations, gather inspiration, create your vision board and update it as your goals change. Remember to be realistic, consistent, and take action towards your goals. A vision board is not a magic wand but a tool to help you on your journey, as ancient philosopher Lao Tzu once said, "The journey of a thousand miles begins with one step." Take that first step towards your vision, and don't let being a lone wolf hold you back. As the ancient Greek philosopher Aristotle said, "Where your talents and the needs of the world cross, there lies your vocation." Trust in yourself and your abilities, and let your vision board be a constant reminder of the person you aspire to be and the life you desire to live. Take inspiration from the greats of ancient civilizations, who also ventured alone on their personal quests for knowledge and fulfillment, such as the famous Chinese philosopher Confucius, who once said, "The will to win, the desire to succeed, the urge to reach your full potential... these are the keys that will unlock the door to personal excellence."

The Power of Positive Thinking

The power of positive thinking is a well-known concept in the world of self-development and personal growth, but what about as a lone wolf? Can one truly harness the power of positive thinking while going it alone? The answer is a resounding yes. In fact, the ability to think positively and maintain a positive mindset is even more crucial for those who choose to go it alone.

For centuries, ancient civilizations have recognized the power of positive thinking and its impact on the individual. The ancient Greek philosopher, Epictetus, once said, "It's not what happens to you, but how you react to it that matters." This statement highlights the importance of our thoughts and reactions in shaping our reality. The Chinese philosopher, Lao Tzu, also recognized the power of positive thinking and stated, "When you change the way you look at things, the things you look at change."

But how exactly can one harness the power of positive thinking as a lone wolf? The key is to focus on the present moment and to cultivate a mindset of gratitude and positivity. When we focus on the present, we are able to let go of negative thoughts and emotions that stem from past experiences or future worries. By cultivating a mindset of gratitude, we are able to shift our focus from what we lack to what we have, which can greatly improve our overall well-being.

One practical way to harness the power of positive thinking as a lone wolf is through journaling. This can be done by writing down three things you are grateful for each day or by keeping a gratitude journal. This simple practice can help shift your focus from negative thoughts and situations to positive ones. It can also help to increase feelings of gratitude and appreciation for what you have in your life.

Another practical way to harness the power of positive thinking as a lone wolf is through visualization. Visualization is the practice of creating mental images of what you want to achieve or experience in your life. This could be visualizing a specific goal you want to achieve, or visualizing a positive outcome in a difficult situation. Visualization can help to increase your motivation and give you a sense of direction and purpose.

Ancient civilizations, such as the Greeks and the Egyptians, believed in the power of positive thinking as well. The Greek philosopher, Epictetus, said "It's not what happens to you, but how you react to it that matters." This quote highlights the importance of how we choose to react to situations and how our thoughts and actions can shape our experiences.

Similarly, the ancient Egyptians believed in the power of positive thinking and the power of the mind to shape reality. They believed that the thoughts and words we speak have the power to create our reality. This belief is reflected in the ancient Egyptian hieroglyph for "word" which depicts a mouth next to a hand holding a tool. This symbolizes the idea that our words have the power to shape and create our reality.

In conclusion, harnessing the power of positive thinking as a lone wolf requires commitment and consistency in practicing techniques such as journaling and visualization. By shifting our focus to positive thoughts and gratitude, we can improve our mental and emotional well-being, increase our motivation and ultimately shape our reality. As the Greek philosopher Aristotle once said, "We are what we repeatedly do. Excellence, then, is not an act, but a habit."

How to Overcome Self-Doubt and Limiting Beliefs

Self-doubt and limiting beliefs are two of the most common obstacles that prevent individuals from reaching their full potential. They can be incredibly detrimental to one's personal and professional development, and can often leave individuals feeling stuck and unmotivated. However, the good news is that it is possible to overcome self-doubt and limiting beliefs, even if you feel like you're a lone wolf.

One of the first steps in overcoming self-doubt and limiting beliefs is to understand what they are and where they come from. Self-doubt is the feeling of uncertainty or lack of confidence in oneself, while limiting beliefs are negative thoughts or perceptions that we hold about ourselves, our abilities, or the world around us. These thoughts and beliefs are often formed in childhood and are reinforced through experiences and interactions with others throughout our lives.

In order to overcome self-doubt and limiting beliefs, it is important to identify and challenge them. One effective way to do this is through self-reflection and journaling. Take some time each day to reflect on your thoughts and beliefs, and write them down. As you do this, pay attention to any negative or limiting thoughts that come up. Once you have identified these thoughts, it is important to challenge and reframe them. For example, if you find yourself thinking "I can't do this," try reframing it to "I can do this, and I will find a way to make it happen."

Another powerful tool for overcoming self-doubt and limiting beliefs is visualization and positive self-talk. Visualization is the practice of creating mental images of yourself achieving your goals and living your desired life. By regularly visualizing yourself in this way, you are training your brain to believe that these things are possible for you. This can help to shift your focus away from your doubts and limiting beliefs, and instead, give you the confidence and motivation you need to take action and make your goals a reality.

Positive self-talk is another important aspect of overcoming self-doubt and limiting beliefs. This refers to the words and phrases you use to talk to yourself on a daily basis. Many of us have a tendency to engage in negative self-talk, which can further fuel our doubts and limiting beliefs. By becoming more aware of the words we use, and actively choosing to use positive, uplifting language, we can begin to shift our mindset and beliefs about ourselves.

One of the key things to remember when it comes to overcoming self-doubt and limiting beliefs is that it's important to be kind and compassionate with yourself. The road to self-discovery and personal growth is not always easy, and there will be setbacks and challenges along the way. But by being patient with yourself, and understanding that progress takes time, you will be better equipped to deal with these obstacles.

For a long time, ancient civilizations have understood the importance of self-talk and visualization. The ancient Egyptians believed that the power of the spoken word could manifest itself in the physical world. They would often recite affirmations and positive affirmations to themselves to manifest their desires. The ancient Greeks also believed in the power of visualization, with the philosopher Aristotle stating, “The soul never thinks without an image”. And the ancient Chinese believed in the power of visualization and positive self-talk as a way to manifest their desires.

Another ancient practice that can be used to overcome self-doubt and limiting beliefs is meditation. Meditation is a powerful tool for quieting the mind and finding inner peace. When we meditate, we focus on our breath, which helps to slow down our racing thoughts and bring us into the present moment. This can be incredibly helpful for those who are struggling with self-doubt and limiting beliefs, as it allows us to step back from our thoughts and see them for what they are – just thoughts, rather than absolute truths.

It is also important to surround yourself with supportive people. Having a support system of people who believe in you and your abilities can be incredibly powerful in helping you to overcome self-doubt and limiting beliefs. They can offer you encouragement and a different perspective when you are feeling down or uncertain.

In conclusion, while self-doubt and limiting beliefs can be incredibly challenging to overcome, it is not impossible. By using the tools and strategies outlined above, such as visualization, positive self-talk, patience and kindness, meditation, and surrounding yourself with supportive people, you can begin to shift your mindset and overcome these barriers that are holding you back. Remember that progress takes time, and be patient and compassionate with yourself as you work through this process. Remember, "The only limit to our realization of tomorrow will be our doubts of today." Franklin D. Roosevelt.

The Role of Action in Achieving Your Vision

As a motivational and self-development expert, I often hear people talk about their visions and goals, but all too often, these visions and goals remain just that: visions and goals. The truth is, having a vision is not enough to achieve success. Action is the key ingredient that turns your vision into reality.

You may be wondering, "What does it mean to be a lone wolf?" A lone wolf is someone who is self-reliant, independent, and driven to achieve their goals without the support of others. It is someone who is comfortable working alone and is not afraid to take risks. In today's world, we often hear the phrase "no man is an island", but the truth is, some people are truly meant to go at it alone.

Many ancient civilizations understood the importance of taking action to achieve one's vision. The ancient Greek philosopher, Aristotle, once said, "Pleasure in the job puts perfection in the work." This quote speaks to the importance of finding joy and purpose in the actions we take towards our goals. The ancient Chinese philosopher, Lao Tzu, also understood the importance of taking action, stating in the Tao Te Ching, "A journey of a thousand miles begins with a single step." This quote reminds us that no matter how daunting a task may seem, it all starts with one small action.

Let's take a look at a practical example of someone who is a lone wolf, Elon Musk. Musk is the founder of Tesla, SpaceX, and Neuralink, among other companies. He is a visionary, and he has a clear vision of where he wants to take his companies and the world. But, it's not just his vision that has made him successful, it's also his action.

Musk has always been a lone wolf in the business world, not afraid to go against the norm and take risks. He is a firm believer in the power of action and has often said, "The first step is to establish that something is possible; then probability will occur."

One of the most notable examples of Musk's ability to turn his vision into action is with SpaceX. Musk's vision was to make space travel more affordable and accessible to the masses. He knew that the key to achieving this was to develop reusable rockets. This was a concept that many experts in the field believed was impossible. But, Musk didn't let that stop him. He took action and poured millions of dollars of his own money into the development of reusable rockets. After years of hard work and setbacks, SpaceX was able to successfully launch and land a reusable rocket in 2015. This achievement was a game changer for the space industry and has paved the way for more affordable and frequent space travel.

Another example is with Tesla, Musk's electric car company. Musk had a vision of a world where electric cars were the norm, and fossil fuels were a thing of the past. This vision was met with skepticism from experts in the car industry. But, Musk didn't let that stop him. He took action and invested his own money into the development of electric cars. Today, Tesla is one of the most successful car companies in the world and has played a significant role in the shift towards electric cars.

The ancient Greek philosopher, Aristotle, once said, "We are what we repeatedly do. Excellence, then, is not an act, but a habit." This quote highlights the importance of action in achieving one's vision. It's not enough to just have a vision, you must also take action to make it a reality.

The ancient Chinese military strategist, Sun Tzu, in his famous work "The Art of War" also emphasized the importance of action. He wrote, "The greatest victory is that which requires no battle." This quote highlights the importance of taking action before your competition does. A lone wolf must be proactive and not wait for opportunities to come to them. They must take action and create opportunities for themselves.

In conclusion, as a lone wolf, it's important to have a clear vision of what you want to achieve and to take action to make it a reality. As Elon Musk has shown, it's not just having a vision that leads to success, it's also taking action to make that vision a reality. As ancient philosophers and strategists have emphasized, it's the combination of vision and action that leads to true excellence. Don't be afraid to be a lone wolf and take risks, as long as you take action, you will be able to achieve your vision.

The Connection Between Visioning and Gratitude

As a motivational and self-development expert, I have come to understand that the connection between visioning and gratitude is an often-overlooked yet powerful combination that can lead to a life of purpose, fulfillment, and abundance. The ability to vision and to be grateful for what we already have is a key aspect of personal growth, and it is especially important for those who choose to walk the path of the lone wolf.

First, let us define what it means to be a lone wolf. A lone wolf is someone who chooses to forge their own path in life, rather than following the crowd. They are independent thinkers and doers who are not afraid to go against the status quo. They are individuals who are comfortable in their own skin, and who have a strong sense of self-worth and purpose.

The ability to vision is an essential aspect of the lone wolf's journey. It is the ability to see beyond the present, to imagine a better future, and to take the necessary steps to make it a reality. Visioning is the process of creating a clear and compelling image of the future that we want to create for ourselves. It is about setting goals and taking action to achieve them. It is about having a sense of purpose and direction in life.

As the Greek philosopher Aristotle once said, "Where there is no vision, the people perish." A clear vision is essential for the lone wolf, as it gives them the direction and motivation they need to keep moving forward, even when the road ahead is difficult. It is the light that guides them on their journey, and it is the beacon that keeps them moving forward, even when all around them seems dark and uncertain.

But what many lone wolves often overlook is the power of gratitude in helping them to achieve their vision. Gratitude is a powerful force that can help to shift our perspective and open our eyes to the blessings and opportunities that are present in our lives, even when we feel like we are alone and struggling.

One of the key benefits of gratitude is that it helps us to see the good in our lives, even when things are not going well. It allows us to appreciate the small moments of joy and contentment that we often take for granted, and it helps us to focus on what we have, rather than what we lack. This can be especially powerful for the lone wolf, who may find themselves feeling isolated and alone, and struggling to find meaning and purpose in their life.

Gratitude can also help to build resilience and inner strength. When we focus on the things we are grateful for, we are less likely to get caught up in negative thoughts and emotions, and more likely to find the strength to keep moving forward, even when things are difficult. This can be especially important for the lone wolf, who may find themselves facing many challenges and obstacles on their journey.

One of the most powerful ways to cultivate gratitude is through the practice of journaling. By taking the time to write down the things we are grateful for each day, we can begin to shift our focus from what is missing in our lives, to what is present and good. This can help us to see the beauty and abundance that is all around us, even when we are feeling alone and disconnected.

Another powerful way to cultivate gratitude is through the practice of mindfulness. By taking the time to be present in the moment and to really pay attention to what is happening around us, we can begin to appreciate the small things in life that we often overlook. This can include the warmth of the sun on our skin, the sound of the birds singing, or the simple pleasure of a good meal.

It is important to note that cultivating gratitude does not mean ignoring or dismissing the difficulties and hardships that we may be facing. Rather, it is about learning to see the good in our lives, even when things are not going well, and to find the strength to keep moving forward, even when we feel alone and disconnected.

The ancient Chinese philosopher Lao Tzu once said, "If you want to awaken all of humanity, then awaken all of yourself." The same is true for the lone wolf. If they want to achieve their vision, they must first awaken the power of gratitude within themselves. They must learn to see the good in their lives, even when things are not going well, and to find the strength to keep moving forward, even when they feel alone and disconnected. In doing so, they will find the motivation and direction they need to achieve their vision, and to live a life that is truly fulfilling and meaningful.

Keeping Your Vision Alive Through Daily Habits

One of the most important daily habits for keeping your vision alive is setting aside time each day for reflection and introspection. This can be as simple as taking a few minutes each morning to sit quietly and reflect on your goals and aspirations. Or, you can use journaling or meditation to explore your thoughts and feelings. Whatever method you choose, it's important to make this time a non-negotiable part of your daily routine.

Another key habit for keeping your vision alive is staying organized and on top of your to-do list. One way to do this is by breaking down your goals into smaller, manageable tasks that you can tackle each day. This not only helps you stay focused on your vision, but it also helps you make steady progress towards your goals.

It's also important to surround yourself with people who support your vision and goals. This might mean seeking out mentors or role models who can guide you on your journey. Or, it could mean joining a group or community of like-minded individuals who share your values and aspirations.

"You are the average of the five people you spend the most time with." - Jim Rohn

Physical activity is also an essential daily habit for keeping your vision alive. Engaging in regular exercise not only improves your physical health, but it also has a positive impact on your mental and emotional well-being. Exercise has been shown to boost self-esteem, reduce stress and anxiety, and improve mood and cognitive function.

To keep your vision alive, it's important to surround yourself with people who uplift, inspire and support you. This means cutting ties with negative or toxic individuals and surrounding yourself with positive, motivated individuals who share similar values and goals.

"You are the average of the five people you spend the most time with." - Jim Rohn

It's also important to set aside time for self-reflection and meditation. Taking time to reflect on your goals, values, and purpose can help keep your vision alive and provide clarity on your path forward. This is also a great time to focus on gratitude and appreciate the present moment.

"The more you know yourself, the more clarity there is. Self-knowledge has no end." - Jiddu Krishnamurti

Another key habit is to consistently work towards achieving your goals. Whether it's through setting small, manageable goals or taking on larger, long-term projects, staying actively engaged in the pursuit of your vision keeps it alive and provides a sense of purpose and direction.

"Your work is going to fill a large part of your life, and the only way to be truly satisfied is to do what you believe is great work. And the only way to do great work is to love what you do." - Steve Jobs

Lastly, reading and learning are also key habits to keeping your vision alive. Reading books, articles, and other materials that align with your values and goals helps to expand your knowledge and understanding, provides inspiration and new perspectives, and keeps you engaged in your personal and professional development.

"The more that you read, the more things you will know. The more that you learn, the more places you'll go." - Dr. Seuss

In summary, keeping your vision alive through daily habits such as surrounding yourself with positive individuals, engaging in physical activity, reflecting on your goals and values, actively pursuing your goals, and consistently learning and expanding your knowledge, can help you stay motivated, focused, and on track to achieving your desired outcomes. Remember that as a lone wolf, it's important to be intentional in your actions, and to be mindful of the company you keep, both in terms of the people in your life and the thoughts that occupy your mind.

The Impact of Community and Support on Visioning.

The impact of community and support on visioning as a lone wolf is often overlooked, but it is one of the most powerful forces in the universe. From ancient civilizations to modern times, history has shown us that when individuals have a strong support system, they are able to achieve great things. In this article, we will explore the importance of community and support in visioning and how it can help individuals achieve their goals, even when they feel like a lone wolf.

First, it is important to understand that visioning is not a solitary process. In fact, it is impossible to vision and create a plan of action alone. We all need support and guidance to help us navigate the twists and turns of life. The ancient Chinese philosopher, Confucius, once said, “The strength of a nation derives from the integrity of the home.” This quote illustrates the importance of community and support in creating a strong foundation for individuals to build upon.

One of the most important aspects of community and support is accountability. When individuals have a support system, they are more likely to be held accountable for their actions. This accountability can come in the form of friends, family, or even a mentor. For example, if an individual has a goal to lose weight, they may join a gym and be held accountable by a personal trainer. This accountability helps the individual stay on track and achieve their goal.

Another important aspect of community and support is the ability to bounce ideas off of others. When individuals are visioning, they often have a lot of ideas and thoughts swirling around in their head. Having a support system allows individuals to share their ideas and get feedback, which can help them to refine and improve upon their vision. This is especially important when it comes to visioning for a business or organization, as it can be difficult to know whether or not a particular idea will be successful without getting input from others.

One of the most famous examples of the power of community and support in visioning comes from the ancient Greek philosopher, Aristotle. He wrote, "The whole is greater than the sum of its parts." This quote highlights the importance of working together as a team, rather than trying to achieve a goal alone. Aristotle recognized that when individuals come together and work towards a common vision, they can accomplish more than they ever could on their own.

Another example comes from the modern business world, where the power of community and support is evident in the success of companies like Apple and Google. These companies are known for fostering a culture of collaboration and innovation, where employees are encouraged to share their ideas and work together to achieve their goals. By creating a supportive environment where individuals can bounce ideas off of each other, these companies have been able to achieve tremendous success.

One of the biggest benefits of having a community and support system is that it can help individuals to stay motivated and focused on their vision. When working alone, it can be easy to become discouraged or lose sight of the bigger picture. However, when individuals have a group of people cheering them on and encouraging them to keep going, they are more likely to stay motivated and see their vision through to the end.

In conclusion, the impact of community and support on visioning is undeniable. Whether it's the ancient Greek philosophers or modern business leaders, it is evident that the power of working together as a team is vital for achieving success. By having a support system in place, individuals can share their ideas, get feedback, and stay motivated on their journey towards achieving their vision. It is important to note that, "Alone we can do so little, together we can do so much" - Helen Keller.

It's important to surround yourself with people who support and believe in you and your vision. They will help you stay focused and motivated, and can provide valuable insights and feedback that can help you refine and improve your ideas. As the ancient Chinese philosopher Lao Tzu said, "A journey of a thousand miles begins with a single step. But with a good support system, that step is much easier to take." So, if you're feeling like a lone wolf, remember the importance of community and support in visioning and work towards building a supportive network that will help you achieve your goals.

Chapter Fourteen: The Importance of Self-Care: Taking Care of Your Physical and Mental Health

Understanding the Connection between Self-Care and Well-Being

Self-care and well-being are two concepts that are often talked about in the same breath, and for good reason. They are closely intertwined and have a significant impact on one another. As a lone wolf, it can be difficult to understand the connection between self-care and well-being, and how to achieve both. However, by understanding the connection and implementing self-care practices, you can improve your well-being and lead a more fulfilling life.

Self-care is the practice of taking care of yourself, both physically and mentally. It includes things like eating well, getting enough sleep, exercising, and taking time for yourself. It also includes practices like mindfulness, meditation, and journaling. Self-care is about taking the time to check in with yourself and make sure that you are taking care of your needs. It's about being kind and compassionate towards yourself, and taking the time to nurture yourself.

Well-being, on the other hand, is the state of being healthy, happy, and content. It encompasses physical, emotional, and mental well-being. When you take care of yourself, you are more likely to feel well and be content. When you are feeling well, you are better able to take care of yourself. It's a cycle that can be difficult to understand, but once you do, it can be a powerful tool for improving your life.

As a lone wolf, it can be difficult to understand the connection between self-care and well-being, and how to achieve both. Society often teaches us that we should be self-sufficient and independent, and that asking for help or support is a sign of weakness. However, this couldn't be further from the truth. In fact, understanding the connection between self-care and well-being is essential for living a fulfilling and successful life, especially as a lone wolf.

Self-care is defined as the actions and practices an individual takes to maintain their physical, mental, and emotional health. This can include things like eating a nutritious diet, getting enough sleep, exercising regularly, and managing stress. On the other hand, well-being is the state of being healthy, happy, and prosperous. It is not just the absence of disease or illness, but a holistic state of overall well-being.

As a lone wolf, it is important to understand that self-care and well-being are not separate entities, but rather they are interconnected and dependent on each other. Self-care is the foundation upon which well-being is built. Without proper self-care, it is impossible to achieve true well-being.

One practical example of this connection can be seen in the ancient practice of yoga. Yoga is a physical and mental discipline that combines movement, breath, and meditation to promote overall well-being. The physical postures, or asanas, are used to strengthen and stretch the body, while the breath work, or pranayama, is used to calm the mind and reduce stress. By practicing yoga, an individual is not only taking care of their physical health, but also their mental and emotional health.

Similarly, in modern day self-care practices, such as journaling or therapy, allows individuals to understand and process their thoughts and emotions, leading to a better understanding of oneself and ultimately leading to better decision making and overall well-being.

The famous philosopher Aristotle once said, "Knowing yourself is the beginning of all wisdom." As a lone wolf, it can be easy to get caught up in the hustle and bustle of daily life and forget to take care of ourselves. But by understanding the connection between self-care and well-being, we can make a conscious effort to prioritize our own needs and make self-care a non-negotiable part of our daily routine.

It's essential to remember that self-care is not selfish, it's necessary. As the ancient Greek physician Hippocrates once said, "Let food be thy medicine and medicine be thy food." This quote emphasizes the importance of taking care of our physical health through proper nutrition and exercise.

As a lone wolf, it's important to remember that self-care doesn't have to be complicated or time-consuming. Simple things like taking a walk outside, reading a book, or even just taking a few deep breaths can have a profound impact on our well-being.

In conclusion, as a lone wolf, it's important to understand the connection between self-care and well-being. By prioritizing our own needs and making self-care a non-negotiable part of our daily routine, we can achieve true well-being and live a fulfilling and successful life. Remember that self-care is not selfish, it's necessary. And as the famous quote by Confucius goes, "The greatest wealth is to live content with little." So, let's make self-care a priority, and live a contented and healthy life.

The Importance of Prioritizing Your Own Health and Wellness

As a lone wolf, it can be easy to get caught up in the hustle and bustle of everyday life and put your own health and wellness on the back burner. Society often teaches us that being self-sufficient and independent means putting others first and neglecting our own needs. But what many don't realize is that prioritizing our own health and wellness is not only crucial for our own happiness and well-being, but it also allows us to better serve and help those around us.

One ancient civilization that understood the importance of self-care was the Greeks. The Greek physician, Hippocrates, famously said "First, do no harm." This statement not only applies to the medical field, but to our overall well-being. In order to truly help and serve others, we must first take care of ourselves. This means not only physically, but emotionally and mentally as well.

In modern times, this concept is echoed by the self-care movement. Self-care is not a luxury, it's a necessity. It means taking the time to nourish our bodies, minds, and spirits. It means being mindful of our own needs and making them a priority. This could be something as simple as taking a relaxing bath before bed, or something more involved like therapy or meditation.

As a lone wolf, it can be easy to fall into the trap of thinking that we don't need anyone else. We can be our own worst enemy, pushing ourselves too hard and not allowing ourselves to rest and recharge. But self-care is not selfish, it's essential. It's about taking the time to understand our own needs and making sure they are met.

One example of this is setting boundaries. As a lone wolf, we may often find ourselves being pulled in multiple directions and feeling the need to please everyone. But this can lead to burnout and neglecting our own needs. Setting boundaries is not about being rude or dismissive, it's about understanding our own limitations and communicating them to others. It's about being honest and transparent with ourselves and others about what we are capable of and what we are not.

Another example of prioritizing our own health and wellness is learning to say no. As a lone wolf, we may often feel the pressure to take on too much and overcommit ourselves. But this can lead to burnout and neglecting our own needs. Learning to say no is not about being rude or dismissive, it's about understanding our own limitations and being honest with ourselves and others about what we are capable of.

The Stoics, another ancient civilization, also understood the importance of self-care and self-awareness. The Stoic philosopher Epictetus said "Know, first, who you are, and then adorn yourself accordingly." This means understanding our own needs and limitations and making sure they are met. It's about being honest with ourselves and others about who we are and what we are capable of.

In conclusion, as a lone wolf, it's essential to understand the connection between self-care and well-being. Prioritizing our own health and wellness is not selfish, it's essential. It's about taking the time to understand our own needs and making sure they are met in order to be the best version of ourselves. It's about setting boundaries and making self-care a non-negotiable part of our daily lives. As ancient philosopher Epictetus once said, "It's not what happens to you, but how you react to it that matters." By prioritizing our own health and wellness, we are better equipped to handle the challenges that come our way and live a fulfilling and meaningful life.

One practical way to prioritize your own health and wellness as a lone wolf is to make a daily self-care routine. This can include things like exercise, meditation, journaling, or even just taking a few minutes to relax and breathe deeply. It's important to find activities that work for you and that you enjoy doing. By making self-care a daily habit, it becomes a non-negotiable part of your life, much like brushing your teeth or eating breakfast.

means going for a hike, taking a walk in the park, or simply sitting and enjoying the beauty of nature.

3. Prioritize self-care activities: Self-care activities can be anything that nourishes the mind, body, and soul. It's important to prioritize self-care activities in your daily routine. These can be things like yoga, meditation, journaling, reading, or taking a relaxing bath. Whatever activities that make you feel good and nourished, make sure you make time for them.

4. Practice mindfulness: Mindfulness is the practice of being present in the moment and fully engaging with one's surroundings. In the digital age, it can be easy to get caught up in the past or the future, and to lose touch with the present moment. Mindfulness practices such as meditation or journaling can help you focus on the present moment, and can be a powerful tool for self-care as a lone wolf.

5. Seek out community: Being a lone wolf doesn't mean you have to be completely isolated. Seek out community by joining groups or organizations that align with your interests and values. This can be in-person or online communities. Having a support system can help you feel less alone and more connected to others.

6. Self-compassion: it is important to be kind and compassionate to oneself. Instead of criticizing oneself, try to practice self-compassion. Self-compassion is being kind and understanding towards oneself during difficult times, rather than being self-critical or judgmental. It's important to remember that as a lone wolf, you are doing the best you can, and that it's okay to not have Self-care is essential for the well-being of any individual, regardless of whether they are a lone wolf or not. However, in the digital age, it can be difficult to practice self-care in a way that truly nourishes the mind, body, and soul. The constant distractions and demands of technology can make it hard to focus on one's own needs, and the sense of isolation that can come from being a lone wolf can make it even harder to take care of oneself.

7. Despite these challenges, it is possible for lone wolves to practice self-care in the digital age. The key is to understand the connection between self-care and well-being, and to make a conscious effort to prioritize self-care in one's daily routine. Here are some practical tips for practicing self-care as a lone wolf in the digital age.

8. Unplug from technology: One of the biggest challenges of self-care in the digital age is the constant distraction and stimulation of technology. One of the best ways to practice self-care as a lone wolf is to take a break from technology and unplug from the constant flow of information. This could mean setting aside time each day to disconnect from your phone, computer, and other digital devices, or it could mean taking a full-fledged digital detox vacation.

9. Connect with nature: Being surrounded by nature can have a profound effect on one's well-being. As a lone wolf, you may feel particularly drawn to the peace and solitude of nature. Take advantage of this by spending time in the great outdoors, whether that means going for a hike, taking a walk in the park, or simply sitting and enjoying the beauty of nature.

10. Prioritize self-care activities: Self-care activities can be anything that nourishes the mind, body, and soul. It's important to prioritize self-care activities in your daily routine. These can be things like yoga, meditation, journaling, reading, or taking a relaxing bath. Whatever activities that make you feel good and nourished, make sure you make time for them.

11. Practice mindfulness: Mindfulness is the practice of being present in the moment and fully engaging with one's surroundings. In the digital age, it can be easy to get caught up in the past or the future, and to lose touch with the present moment. Mindfulness practices such as meditation or journaling can help you focus on the present moment, and can be a powerful tool for self-care as a lone wolf.

12. Seek out community: Being a lone wolf doesn't mean you have to be completely isolated. Seek out community by joining groups or organizations that align with your interests and values. This can be in-person or online communities. Having a support system can help you feel less alone and more connected to others.

13. Self-compassion: it is important to be kind and compassionate to oneself. Instead of criticizing oneself, try to practice self-compassion. Self-compassion is being kind and understanding towards oneself during difficult times, rather than being self-critical or judgmental. It's important to remember that as a lone wolf, you are doing the best you can, and that it's okay to not have

The Impact of Stress on Physical and Mental Health

As a lone wolf, it is important to understand the impact of stress on both physical and mental health. Stress is a natural response to challenges and pressures in life, but when it becomes chronic, it can have serious consequences on our well-being.

One of the most significant impacts of stress on physical health is the risk of developing cardiovascular disease. Stress triggers the release of hormones such as adrenaline and cortisol, which increase heart rate and blood pressure. Over time, this can cause damage to the blood vessels and the heart, increasing the risk of heart attacks and strokes.

In addition to cardiovascular disease, stress can also contribute to the development of other chronic health conditions such as diabetes, obesity, and digestive problems. Stress can also weaken the immune system, making it more difficult to fight off infections and illnesses.

The impact of stress on mental health is just as significant. Chronic stress can lead to a wide range of emotional and psychological problems, such as anxiety, depression, and irritability. Stress can also make it more difficult to concentrate and make decisions, and can lead to feelings of hopelessness and helplessness.

As a lone wolf, it can be especially challenging to manage stress, as we may not have the same support systems and networks as others. However, there are several strategies that can help to minimize the impact of stress on physical and mental health.

One of the most effective ways to manage stress is through regular exercise. Physical activity releases endorphins, which are natural mood-boosters that can help to reduce feelings of anxiety and depression. Exercise can also improve sleep, which is essential for maintaining overall health and well-being.

Another important strategy for managing stress is to practice mindfulness and meditation. These practices can help to quiet the mind, reduce feelings of stress and anxiety, and improve overall well-being.

It is also important to take care of yourself by eating well, getting enough sleep, and taking time to relax and unwind. It is easy to neglect self-care when stress is high, but it is more important than ever to prioritize self-care during times of stress.

As the famous author and speaker, Louise Hay said, "The highest form of self-care is self-love". We must learn to love ourselves and take care of ourselves, as we are the only ones who will be there for us throughout our entire lives.

In conclusion, as a lone wolf, it is important to understand the impact of stress on physical and mental health and take steps to manage it effectively. By exercising, practicing mindfulness and meditation, eating well, getting enough sleep, and taking time to relax and unwind, we can minimize the negative impact of stress and improve our overall well-being.

Making Time for Self-Care in a Busy Schedule

Self-care is often viewed as a luxury that we don't have time for in our busy schedules, but as a lone wolf, it is essential to our well-being. The truth is, making time for self-care is not a matter of finding more hours in a day, but rather, a matter of shifting our priorities. In order to truly take care of ourselves, we need to see self-care as a non-negotiable, just like our work and other responsibilities.

One of the biggest obstacles to self-care is the belief that it has to be done in one big chunk of time. We often think of self-care as going to a spa for a full day, or taking a week-long yoga retreat. However, this is not the case. Self-care can be done in small, manageable chunks of time. For example, taking a five-minute break to do some deep breathing exercises or stretching, or taking a ten-minute walk during lunch. These small moments of self-care can add up and make a big difference in our overall well-being.

Another obstacle to self-care is the belief that it is selfish. As a lone wolf, it can be easy to put the needs of others before our own. We may feel guilty for taking time for ourselves, or that we are neglecting our responsibilities. However, this could not be further from the truth. Self-care is not selfish, it is essential. When we take care of ourselves, we are better equipped to take care of others. As author and speaker Brené Brown says, "Self-care is giving the world the best of you, instead of what's left of you."

In addition to shifting our beliefs about self-care, we can also make time for it by being intentional about how we spend our time. This means setting boundaries and saying no to things that don't serve us. It also means being mindful about how we spend our time, and making sure that we are not filling it with things that are not important to us.

One effective way to make time for self-care is to schedule it into our day. This means setting aside specific times for self-care activities, just like we would with any other appointment. For example, setting aside 30 minutes in the morning for meditation, or 15 minutes before bed for journaling. By scheduling self-care into our day, we are making it a priority and ensuring that we make time for it.

It is also essential to find activities that we enjoy and that make us feel good. Self-care is not about doing things that we don't want to do, it is about doing things that make us feel good. This may mean different things for different people, but it could be anything from going for a run, reading a book, taking a bath, listening to music, cooking, or even just sitting in silence.

Self-care is an essential practice for any lone wolf, and it is vital for maintaining our well-being. By shifting our beliefs about self-care, being intentional about how we spend our time, and scheduling it into our day, we can make time for self-care in our busy schedules. And by engaging in self-care, we can improve our overall well-being, increase our resilience, and achieve greater balance in our lives.

One of the biggest misconceptions about self-care is that it is a luxury, something that can only be done when we have free time. However, self-care is not a luxury, it is a necessity. As renowned author and motivational speaker, Brené Brown, states, "Self-care is not self-indulgence, it is self-preservation."

In order to make time for self-care in our busy schedules, we must first shift our mindset. Instead of viewing self-care as something that is optional, we must recognize it as an essential part of our daily routine. This means being intentional about how we spend our time and making self-care a priority.

One practical way to make time for self-care is by scheduling it into our day. This can be done by setting aside specific time each day for self-care activities, such as reading, meditating, or going for a walk. Another way to make time for self-care is by integrating it into our daily routines. For example, instead of spending our lunch break scrolling through social media, we can use that time to take a walk or read a book.

Another important aspect of making time for self-care is being mindful of how we spend our time. This means being aware of the activities that drain our energy and limit our ability to engage in self-care, and making the conscious decision to limit or eliminate those activities. This may mean saying no to social invitations, or setting boundaries with work or family obligations.

It's also important to remember that self-care can take many different forms, and it's important to find activities that work for you. For some, self-care may mean going for a run, for others it may be taking a hot bath, and for others it may be spending time in nature. The key is to find activities that nourish your soul, and make you feel good.

One of the great modern author and speaker, Tim Ferriss said "Self-care is how you take your power back." It's important to remember that self-care is not selfish, it's self-preservation. By taking the time to care for ourselves, we're better equipped to handle the demands of daily life, and to be there for others when they need us.

In conclusion, making time for self-care in a busy schedule as a lone wolf requires shifting our beliefs, being intentional about how we spend our time, and making self-care a priority. By engaging in self-care, we can improve our overall well-being, increase our resilience and achieve greater balance in our lives. Remember, self-care is not a luxury, it's a necessity, and it's essential for maintaining our mental and physical health as we navigate life's challenges.

It's important to remember that self-care is not selfish, it's self-preservation. As the famous author and speaker Brené Brown once said, "Self-care is giving the world the best of you, instead of what's left of you." By taking care of ourselves, we are better equipped to take care of others and to fulfill our responsibilities.

Another modern author, Gretchen Rubin, in her book "The Four Tendencies" suggests that we can make self-care a habit by identifying our personal tendency and creating an environment that supports our self-care routine. For example, if you're an Upholder, you're likely to be highly disciplined and can set a schedule for yourself, if you're a Questioner, you might need to understand the reasons behind the self-care practice before committing to it, if you're a Rebel, you might want to make self-care fun and non-conventional, if you're an Obliger, you might need an accountability partner or a group to join.

It's essential to remember that self-care is not a one-time event or a luxury, it's a daily practice and a lifestyle. As the ancient Chinese philosopher Lao Tzu said, "The best time to plant a tree was 20 years ago. The second best time is now." It's never too late to start prioritizing self-care and making it a part of your daily routine.

In summary, making time for self-care in a busy schedule as a lone wolf requires shifting our beliefs, being intentional about how we spend our time, and making self-care a priority. By understanding our personal tendencies, creating an environment that supports our self-care routine and making it a daily practice and a lifestyle, we can achieve greater balance in our lives and improve our overall well-being.

The Role of Mindfulness in Self-Care

As a lone wolf, it can be challenging to maintain a healthy balance between self-care and the demands of daily life. The constant pull of responsibilities, relationships, and career can make it difficult to prioritize our own well-being. However, one key aspect to self-care that often goes overlooked is the practice of mindfulness.

Mindfulness is the act of being present in the moment, fully engaged in the here and now. It is about paying attention to our thoughts, feelings, and physical sensations without judgment. Mindfulness has been shown to improve mental and physical health, reduce stress, and increase overall well-being.

One of the most common misconceptions about mindfulness is that it requires a significant time commitment or specific lifestyle changes. However, the beauty of mindfulness is that it can be practiced anywhere, at any time. It can be as simple as taking a few deep breaths before a meeting or pausing to savor a meal.

Lone wolves, who often have a tendency to isolate themselves and push away emotions, can particularly benefit from mindfulness practices as it allows them to be present with and acknowledge their own thoughts and feelings. Mindfulness can provide a sense of inner peace and calmness, allowing lone wolves to be more in tune with their own needs and to be better equipped to make decisions that are in alignment with those needs.

As a lone wolf, it can be easy to fall into the trap of constantly pushing ourselves to achieve more and be more, without taking the time to check in with ourselves and our own well-being. Mindfulness provides an opportunity to step back and take stock of our own needs, to be present with ourselves and our own thoughts and feelings.

"Mindfulness is like a microscope; it is neither an offensive nor a defensive weapon in relation to the germs we observe through it. The function of the microscope is just to clearly present what is there" - Jon Kabat-Zinn, an American professor emeritus of medicine and the creator of the Stress Reduction Clinic and the Center for Mindfulness in Medicine, Health Care, and Society at the University of Massachusetts Medical School

One practical way to integrate mindfulness into daily life as a lone wolf is to set aside a few minutes each day for a mindfulness practice, such as meditation or mindful breathing. There are many resources available, such as apps and guided meditations, to help with this practice. It's also important to find activities that bring joy and relaxation, such as yoga, reading or taking nature walks.

Another way to integrate mindfulness into daily life is to practice mindfulness during daily activities, such as eating, showering, and even when doing chores. For example, when washing the dishes, focus on the sensation of the water on the skin, the smell of the soap, and the movement of the hands. Engage all the senses and be fully present in the moment.

"The greatest weapon against stress is our ability to choose one thought over another" - William James, an American philosopher, psychologist, and physician who is considered to be the father of American psychology

In conclusion, as a lone wolf, it is easy to get caught up in the demands of daily life and neglect our own well-being. Mindfulness can provide a powerful tool for self-care by helping us to understand and acknowledge our thoughts and emotions, and to respond to them in a more intentional and compassionate way. By practicing mindfulness, we can learn to be more present in the moment, to let go of unproductive thoughts and emotions, and to cultivate a sense of inner peace and balance.

One of the key ways that mindfulness can help us to take care of ourselves is by bringing us back to the present moment. When we are caught up in our thoughts and emotions, we can become disconnected from our bodies and the present moment. Mindfulness practices, such as mindful breathing, can help to anchor us in the present and to cultivate a sense of inner calm and focus.

Mindfulness can also help us to let go of negative thoughts and emotions that can be detrimental to our well-being. When we become aware of thoughts and emotions that are harmful to us, we can choose to let them go, rather than getting caught up in them and allowing them to take over. This can help to reduce feelings of stress and anxiety, and to improve our overall well-being.

Additionally, mindfulness can help us to develop a more compassionate and understanding approach to our thoughts and emotions. When we become more aware of our inner experience, we can learn to be more kind and understanding towards ourselves, rather than judging ourselves harshly. This can help to improve our self-esteem and self-worth, and to foster a greater sense of inner peace and contentment.

One author who emphasizes the importance of mindfulness in self-care is Jon Kabat-Zinn, who wrote "Wherever you go, there you are: mindfulness meditation in everyday life". He states that "Mindfulness practice means that we commit fully in each moment to be present; inviting ourselves to interface with this moment in full awareness, with the intention to embody as best we can an orientation of calmness, mindfulness, and equanimity right here and right now."

Another author, Thich Nhat Hanh, in his book "The Sun My Heart" wrote "When we are mindful, deeply in touch with the present moment, our understanding of what is going on deepens, and we begin to be filled with acceptance, joy, peace and love."

In conclusion, as a lone wolf, self-care can be a challenge, but it is an essential aspect of well-being. Mindfulness offers a powerful tool for self-care, allowing us to connect with the present moment, let go of negative thoughts and emotions, and develop a more compassionate and understanding approach to our inner experience. By incorporating mindfulness practices into our daily routine, we can improve our overall well-being and lead a more fulfilling life.

The Importance of Self-Care for Long-Term Health and Happiness

Self-care is often seen as a luxury, something that can be put off until later or only practiced by those who have the time and resources. However, as a lone wolf, it is essential to understand that self-care is not just a nice-to-have, but a necessity for long-term health and happiness.

Many of us have been taught that self-care is selfish, that it is a sign of weakness to take time for ourselves. But in reality, self-care is an act of self-love and self-compassion. It is about taking the time to nurture and nourish ourselves, both physically and emotionally. When we practice self-care, we are saying to ourselves that we are worthy of care and attention, that we deserve to be treated well.

Self-care is not just about bubble baths and spa days, it is about the daily practices that help us to maintain our physical, emotional and mental well-being. It is about eating well, getting enough sleep, exercising, and managing stress. It is about setting boundaries, learning to say no, and taking time to engage in activities that bring us joy. It is about being mindful of our thoughts and emotions and seeking help when we need it.

For lone wolves, self-care is especially important. Without the support and companionship of others, it can be easy to neglect our own needs and become isolated. We may find ourselves constantly giving to others, without taking time to replenish our own energy. This can lead to burnout, and to a host of physical and emotional health problems.

However, self-care can be difficult to practice, especially for lone wolves who may not have a support system in place. It can be hard to know where to start, or to make the time for self-care when we are already stretched thin. But it is important to remember that self-care is not a one-time event, it is a daily practice. It is about making small changes, and being kind and patient with ourselves.

One practical way to practice self-care as a lone wolf is by setting aside a specific time each day to focus on yourself. This can be as simple as taking a few minutes to meditate, or to journal about your thoughts and emotions. It can also be taking a walk, reading a book, or engaging in a hobby. The key is to make this time non-negotiable, and to commit to it each day.

Another way to practice self-care is by building a support system, even if it is not a traditional one. This can be done by reaching out to friends, family or a therapist for emotional support. It can also be about connecting with others through a community or a support group. By building a network of people who understand and support us, we can feel less alone and more supported in our journey towards self-care.

It is also important to practice self-compassion as a lone wolf. Instead of being hard on ourselves, we should be kind and patient with ourselves. We should remind ourselves that we are doing the best we can with the resources we have. We should also remind ourselves that we are not alone, and that there are others who care about us and want to support us.

As a lone wolf, it can be easy to fall into the trap of constantly pushing ourselves to be the best, to achieve more, and to never rest. But this mentality can lead to burnout, exhaustion, and ultimately, long-term health problems. It's important to remember that self-care is not selfish, it's essential for our well-being and longevity.

One practical way to practice self-care as a lone wolf is to make time for activities that bring us joy and relaxation. This can be anything from reading a book, taking a walk in nature, or practicing yoga. It's important to find activities that nourish our mind, body, and soul and make them a regular part of our routine.

Another important aspect of self-care as a lone wolf is to surround ourselves with supportive and positive people. This can be in the form of friends, family, or a therapist. It's important to have a support system in place to help us navigate the ups and downs of life. It's also important to remember that as a lone wolf, we have the power to create our own community and surround ourselves with people who lift us up and make us feel good about ourselves.

In the words of author Brené Brown, "Self-care is giving the world the best of you, instead of what's left of you." It's important to remember that by taking care of ourselves, we are better equipped to take care of others and make a positive impact on the world.

As a lone wolf, it can be easy to fall into the trap of feeling isolated and alone, but self-care can help us remember that we are not alone in our struggles and that there is always hope for a brighter future. As modern author, Matt Haig reminds us, "Self-care is not self-indulgence, it is self-preservation." It's important to remember that self-care is not only essential for our well-being, but also crucial for our survival as a lone wolf.

In conclusion, as a lone wolf, it's essential to understand the connection between self-care and well-being and make it a priority in our daily lives. By making time for activities that bring us joy, surrounding ourselves with supportive people, and practicing self-compassion, we can achieve long-term health and happiness. Remember, as modern author, Audre Lorde said, "Caring for myself is not self-indulgence, it is self-preservation and that is an act of political warfare." Taking care of ourselves is not only important for our individual well-being, but also for our ability to make a positive impact on the world.

How to Create a Self-Care Routine that Works for You.

As a lone wolf, it can be challenging to understand the importance of self-care and how to create a routine that works for you. Society often teaches us that we should be self-sufficient and independent, and that taking care of ourselves is a luxury or a weakness. However, nothing could be further from the truth. Taking care of ourselves is essential to our overall well-being, and it is a form of self-love and self-respect that is vital to our survival.

Self-care is not just about pampering ourselves or indulging in luxurious activities, it is about creating a balance between our physical, emotional, and mental well-being. It is about taking the time to listen to our bodies and minds, and understanding what we need to feel our best.

The first step in creating a self-care routine that works for you as a lone wolf is to understand your needs. Each person is unique, and what works for one person may not work for another. It is important to take the time to reflect on what you need to feel your best. This may involve journaling, meditation, or talking to a therapist or coach.

Once you have a better understanding of your needs, it is time to create a self-care routine that works for you. This will likely involve a combination of different activities, including physical exercise, healthy eating, rest, relaxation, and mental and emotional self-care.

Physical exercise is an essential component of self-care. It not only helps to improve our physical health, but it also has a positive impact on our mental and emotional well-being. Whether it is running, yoga, or weightlifting, finding an exercise routine that works for you can help to reduce stress, improve mood, and boost self-esteem.

Eating a healthy diet is another important aspect of self-care. As a lone wolf, it can be easy to fall into the trap of eating processed foods or relying on takeout. However, a diet rich in fruits, vegetables, and lean protein can help to improve our overall health and well-being.

Rest and relaxation are also important components of self-care. This can include activities such as reading, journaling, taking a bath, or listening to music. It is essential to take the time to unwind and disconnect from the stresses of daily life.

Mental and emotional self-care is also essential. This can include activities such as therapy, journaling, or talking to a coach or mentor. It is important to take the time to process our thoughts and feelings, and to seek support when needed.

Creating a self-care routine that works for you as a lone wolf may take some trial and error. It is important to be patient with yourself and to understand that it may take time to find what works best for you. However, once you have found a routine that works, you will find that it is easier to maintain and will help you to feel your best.

As author and motivational speaker Brené Brown said, "Self-care is not self-indulgence, it is self-preservation." As a lone wolf, it is essential to understand the importance of self -care and how to create a routine that works for you.

First and foremost, it's important to recognize that self-care looks different for everyone. Some people may find solace in yoga and meditation, while others may find it in going for a run or listening to music. The key is to find what works for you and make it a consistent part of your routine.

One way to create a self-care routine that works for you is to start by identifying your needs. Are you feeling stressed and in need of relaxation? Are you feeling lonely and in need of social interaction? Are you feeling physically exhausted and in need of rest? By identifying your needs, you can tailor your self-care routine to address them.

Another important aspect of self-care is setting boundaries. As a lone wolf, it can be easy to overextend yourself and neglect your own needs. But in order to truly take care of yourself, it's important to set boundaries and say "no" when necessary. This could mean setting limits on your workload, or setting boundaries with friends or family.

Another way to create a self-care routine that works for you is to make it a priority. This means setting aside time each day or each week to focus on yourself and your needs. It could be as simple as taking a few minutes each day to meditate or journal, or setting aside an hour each week to do something you enjoy.

Incorporating self-care activities that align with your values, such as volunteering, giving back to the community, or pursuing a passion project can also be a great way to improve well-being as a lone wolf. This can help to give a sense of purpose and fulfillment that goes beyond the self.

It's also important to remember that self-care is not just about physical well-being, but also emotional and mental well-being. This means taking care of your emotional and mental health by seeking out therapy or counseling, connecting with friends and loved ones, and practicing mindfulness and gratitude.

Furthermore, self-care also means being aware of your thoughts and patterns and challenging negative and self-defeating thoughts. To quote author and speaker Tony Robbins "It's not the events of our lives that shape us, but our beliefs as to what those events mean."

In conclusion, self-care as a lone wolf is crucial for maintaining a balance and well-being, but it is not always easy to achieve. It takes time, effort, and commitment to create a self-care routine that works for you. Remember to identify your needs, set boundaries, make self-care a priority, align your values, and take care of your emotional and mental well-being. Remember, as author and poet Maya Angelou said, "I take care of myself so well that when others see me, they are inspired to do the same." Be kind to yourself and never underestimate the power of self-care. It can help you to be more resilient, focused, and fulfilled as a lone wolf. It can help you to build a better relationship with yourself and to create a life that you truly love and enjoy. Remember, you are in charge of your own well-being, and it is never too late to start taking care of yourself. Take the first step today, and see the positive changes that self-care can bring to your life as a lone wolf.

Chapter Fifteen: Building a Positive Mindset: Harnessing the Power of Positive Thinking

Understanding the Science of Positive Thinking

As a lone wolf, it can be easy to fall into the trap of negative thinking and self-doubt. However, understanding the science behind positive thinking can help you to break free from these limiting beliefs and achieve greater well-being.

The power of positive thinking has been well-documented in scientific literature. Studies have shown that people who think positively experience a host of benefits, including increased optimism, better physical health, and improved relationships. In fact, one study found that people who practiced positive thinking had a 29% lower risk of developing depression and a 14% lower risk of developing heart disease.

So how exactly does positive thinking work? One key component is the concept of neuroplasticity, which refers to the brain's ability to change and adapt in response to new information. When we think positively, we are actually rewiring our brain to focus on the positive aspects of our lives, rather than dwelling on negative thoughts and experiences.

One practical example of harnessing the power of positive thinking is through the use of affirmations. Affirmations are positive statements that can be repeated to oneself on a daily basis, such as "I am confident and capable" or "I am surrounded by love and support." These affirmations have been shown to help people change negative thought patterns and boost self-esteem.

Another effective technique for promoting positive thinking is the practice of gratitude. By focusing on the things in our lives that we are grateful for, we can shift our perspective from one of lack and scarcity to one of abundance and contentment. This can be done through journaling, talking to a friend, or even just taking a moment each day to reflect on the things we are thankful for.

It's also important to understand that positive thinking isn't always easy, and that it's normal to experience setbacks and negative thoughts. The key is to not let these moments define us, but rather to use them as opportunities to learn and grow.

In the words of modern author Louise Hay, "The thoughts we choose to think are the tools we use to paint the canvas of our lives." As a lone wolf, it can be easy to feel isolated and disconnected. But by understanding the science behind positive thinking, you can empower yourself to create a life that is rich, fulfilling, and full of joy.

Modern author Dr Wayne Dyer said "Change the way you look at things and the things you look at change." By changing our perspective and focusing on the positive, we can tap into our inner strength and resilience, and create a life that is truly worth living.

It's important to remember that self-care and positive thinking go hand in hand. Without taking care of ourselves, it's hard to maintain a positive outlook. It's important to make time for ourselves, whether it's through exercise, meditation, or simply taking a relaxing bath. By taking care of ourselves physically, emotionally and mentally, we're better equipped to handle the ups and downs of life with a positive attitude.

In conclusion, understanding the science of positive thinking as a lone wolf is essential to achieving well-being. By rewiring our brain to focus on the positive, practicing gratitude, and taking care of ourselves, we can break free from negative thought patterns and embrace a more fulfilling life.

It's easy to fall into the trap of thinking that being a lone wolf means we have to go through life alone, without support or connection. However, this couldn't be further from the truth. Positive thinking allows us to build connections with ourselves and others, and to find joy and purpose in our lives.

So, as a lone wolf, embrace the power of positive thinking. Cultivate gratitude, focus on the good things in your life, and take care of yourself. Remember, as the author Norman Vincent Peale once said, "Change your thoughts and you change your world." With positive thinking as your guide, you can create the life you want and become the person you were meant to be.

Harnessing the Power of Positive Affirmations

As a lone wolf, harnessing the power of positive affirmations can seem like a daunting task. Society often teaches us to be self-sufficient and independent, and the idea of repeating positive phrases to ourselves can feel foreign and uncomfortable. However, the truth is that positive affirmations are a powerful tool for personal growth and can have a profound impact on our well-being as a lone wolf.

Positive affirmations are simple, positive statements that we repeat to ourselves on a daily basis. These statements can be about anything, from our self-worth to our career aspirations. The purpose of affirmations is to help us focus on the positive aspects of our lives and to change the way we think and feel about ourselves and our circumstances.

One of the biggest benefits of using positive affirmations as a lone wolf is that they can help us to shift our mindset from negative to positive. As a lone wolf, it can be easy to fall into the trap of negative self-talk, constantly criticizing ourselves and focusing on our shortcomings. By repeating positive affirmations, we can start to change the way we think and feel about ourselves, and begin to see ourselves in a more positive light.

Another benefit of using positive affirmations as a lone wolf is that they can help us to achieve our goals. When we repeat positive affirmations, we are essentially programming our minds to believe in the things we are saying. This can help us to overcome self-doubt and fear, and give us the confidence and motivation we need to pursue our goals.

Using positive affirmations as a lone wolf can also have a profound impact on our physical and emotional well-being. Research has shown that positive affirmations can help to reduce stress, improve mood, and boost self-esteem. This can have a positive impact on our physical health, as well as our mental and emotional well-being.

One of the most important things to remember when using positive affirmations as a lone wolf is to be consistent. In order for affirmations to be effective, we need to repeat them on a regular basis. This can be done by setting aside a few minutes each day to focus on our affirmations, or by writing them down and placing them in a visible location where we will see them often.

It is also important to make sure that our affirmations are realistic and achievable. The statements we make should be something that we truly believe in and that we can work towards. It is also important to make sure that our affirmations are in the present tense, as this helps to create a sense of immediacy and urgency.

"The power of positive affirmations is that it can change the way you think, and when you change the way you think, you change the way you feel" - Tony Robbins

"Affirmations are like seeds, planted in the soil of the mind, that will grow and bloom into beautiful reality" - Louise Hay

"Positive affirmations are a simple, yet powerful tool that can change the way you think, feel and behave" - Rhonda Byrne

In conclusion, as a lone wolf, harnessing the power of positive affirmations can seem intimidating at first. But by understanding the connection between self-care and well- being, and the role that our thoughts and beliefs play in shaping our reality, we can begin to see the true potential of these simple yet powerful tools. Positive affirmations can help us to tap into our inner strength and resilience, and to overcome the limiting beliefs and negative self-talk that can hold us back. They can also help us to cultivate a sense of self-worth and self-love, and to manifest the life that we truly desire.

It's important to note that positive affirmations are not a magic solution, and they won't solve all of our problems overnight. But with consistent practice, they can help us to shift our mindset, and to develop a more positive and empowering perspective on life.

As the author Louise Hay once said, "Affirmations are like seeds. When we plant them in the soil of our consciousness, they begin to grow and take root, and eventually, they will blossom into reality."

Another great example is the author and motivational speaker Tony Robbins, who states "The only limit to our realization of tomorrow will be our doubts of today.".

By taking the time to practice positive affirmations on a daily basis, we can begin to see a real difference in our thoughts, feelings, and actions. We can also start to develop a deeper understanding of the connection between self-care and well-being as a lone wolf. So, if you're ready to take charge of your life and start living to your full potential, give positive affirmations a try. You may just be surprised at the positive changes that you can achieve.

Creating a Positive Mindset: Techniques and Strategies

As a lone wolf, it is essential to create and maintain a positive mindset in order to achieve success and happiness in life. However, this can be easier said than done, especially when facing challenges and obstacles alone. But with the right techniques and strategies, it is possible to develop a positive mindset that will empower you to overcome any obstacle and achieve your goals.

One of the most important things to understand is that our thoughts and beliefs shape our reality. If we constantly focus on negative thoughts and beliefs, we will attract negative experiences and outcomes in our lives. But if we focus on positive thoughts and beliefs, we will attract positive experiences and outcomes. Therefore, one of the key strategies for creating a positive mindset is to actively work on shifting our thoughts and beliefs to a more positive perspective.

One technique that can be helpful in this regard is visualization. Visualization is the act of creating mental images of the things we want to achieve or the life we want to live. By visualizing ourselves in a positive state, we can begin to shift our thoughts and beliefs to align with that positive reality. This can be done by setting aside time each day to close your eyes and visualize yourself in a positive state, such as achieving a goal or living a happy and fulfilled life.

Another technique that can be beneficial for creating a positive mindset is to practice gratitude. Gratitude is the act of being thankful for the things we have in our lives. When we focus on the things we are grateful for, we shift our attention away from negative thoughts and towards positive ones. This can be done by keeping a gratitude journal, where you write down things you are grateful for each day, or by simply taking a few moments each day to reflect on the things you are grateful for.

Another key strategy for creating a positive mindset is to surround yourself with positive influences. This includes the people you spend time with, the media you consume, and the environments you find yourself in. Be intentional about spending time with people who are positive, supportive, and uplifting. Avoid those who are negative and draining. Also, limit your exposure to negative news and media, and instead seek out positive and uplifting content.

It is also important to practice self-care as a lone wolf. Self-care is the act of taking care of your physical, emotional, and mental well-being. This includes things like exercise, healthy eating, getting enough sleep, and taking time to relax and unwind. When we practice self-care, we are better able to cope with stress and negative thoughts, and we are more likely to have a positive mindset.

Lastly, one important aspect to consider in creating a positive mindset is to practice mindfulness. Mindfulness is the act of being present and aware in the moment. This means paying attention to your thoughts, feelings, and bodily sensations without judging them. By practicing mindfulness, we can become more aware of our thoughts and beliefs, and we can more easily shift them to a more positive perspective.

In conclusion, as a lone wolf, creating a positive mindset is essential to achieving success and happiness in life. By utilizing techniques such as visualization, gratitude, surrounding yourself with positive influences, self-care and mindfulness, you can shift your thoughts and beliefs to a more positive and empowering place. The key to success is to consistently practice these techniques and strategies, making them a habit in your daily life.

One modern author, Louise Hay, once said, "The thoughts we choose to think are the tools we use to paint the canvas of our lives." This quote highlights the power of our thoughts and the impact they have on our lives. By actively choosing to think positively, we can shape our reality and manifest the life we desire.

Another author, Tony Robbins, also emphasizes the importance of shifting our mindset, stating, "It is not what we get, but who we become, what we contribute... that gives meaning to our lives." This quote reminds us that true fulfillment and happiness come from becoming the best version of ourselves and making a positive impact on others.

As a lone wolf, it is important to remember that you are not alone in your journey towards creating a positive mindset. There are countless resources and support systems available to help guide and support you. Whether it be through therapy, self-help books, or personal development workshops, seeking out these resources can provide valuable insight and tools to help you on your journey.

It is also important to remember that progress and growth are not linear. There will be setbacks and challenges along the way, but it is crucial to not let these setbacks discourage you. Instead, view them as opportunities for growth and learning. As the author and speaker, Brené Brown, said, "Vulnerability is the birthplace of innovation, creativity and change." Embracing vulnerability and facing challenges head-on can lead to personal growth and a deeper understanding of oneself.

In summary, as a lone wolf, creating a positive mindset is essential to achieving success and happiness in life. By utilizing techniques such as visualization, gratitude, surrounding yourself with positive influences, self-care and mindfulness, you can shift your thoughts and beliefs to a more positive and empowering place. Remember that progress and growth are not linear and that seeking out resources and support can help guide and support you on your journey. Embrace vulnerability and view challenges as opportunities for growth and learning. With a positive mindset, you can manifest the life you desire and become the best version of yourself.

Building Resilience: Coping with Setbacks and Failure

Building resilience is the key to coping with setbacks and failure in life. Many people believe that resilience is something that you are born with, but the truth is that it can be developed and strengthened over time. Resilience is the ability to bounce back from difficult situations, to adapt and grow from challenges, and to keep moving forward even in the face of adversity.

One of the most important things to understand about resilience is that it is not about avoiding failure or setbacks altogether. Instead, it is about how you respond to these challenges when they inevitably arise. When you build resilience, you are preparing yourself to handle difficult situations in a way that allows you to come out stronger on the other side.

One of the most effective ways to build resilience is through mindfulness and self-reflection. This means taking the time to reflect on your thoughts, feelings, and behaviors, and to understand how they are impacting your ability to cope with difficult situations. By developing a deeper understanding of yourself and your reactions to stress, you can begin to identify patterns and triggers that are holding you back.

Another important aspect of building resilience is learning to let go of perfectionism. Perfectionism is the belief that you must always be perfect, and that anything less than perfection is failure. This can be incredibly damaging, as it sets you up for constant disappointment and failure. Instead, you must learn to accept that failure is a natural and necessary part of life, and that it can be a valuable learning experience.

Another key to building resilience is learning to find meaning and purpose in difficult situations. When you are able to find a sense of purpose and meaning in your struggles, you are better able to cope with them. This may involve reframing the way you think about your challenges, or finding ways to use them as an opportunity for growth and development.

Finally, building resilience also requires developing a support system of friends, family, and community. In difficult times, it's important to have people you can turn to for support and guidance. Surrounding yourself with positive and supportive people can help you to cope with setbacks and failure, and to find the strength to keep going.

In conclusion, building resilience is not about avoiding failure or setbacks, but rather learning to cope with them in a way that allows you to come out stronger on the other side. By developing mindfulness and self-reflection, letting go of perfectionism, finding meaning and purpose in difficult situations, and building a support system, you can build resilience and become better equipped to handle whatever life throws your way. Remember that failure is not the opposite of success, but rather a stepping stone towards it. As the famous quote says "Fall seven times, stand up eight" - Japanese Proverb.

The Power of Positive Thinking in Achieving Goals and Dreams.

The power of positive thinking is often overlooked in our fast-paced, results-driven society. However, the truth is that our thoughts have a profound impact on our ability to achieve our goals and dreams. As a renowned self-help author, I have seen time and time again how a positive mindset can help individuals overcome seemingly insurmountable obstacles and achieve success in every area of their lives.

One of the most powerful benefits of positive thinking is that it helps us to focus on solutions, rather than problems. When we are mired in negative thoughts, we tend to see only the difficulties and challenges that stand in our way. But when we shift our focus to positive thoughts, we begin to see opportunities and possibilities that we never noticed before. This shift in perspective gives us the energy and motivation we need to take action and make progress towards our goals.

Positive thinking also helps us to build resilience in the face of adversity. When we are faced with setbacks or disappointments, it is easy to become discouraged and give up. But when we have a positive mindset, we are better able to bounce back from these challenges and keep moving forward. This is because positive thinking helps us to see the silver lining in every situation and to find the lessons and opportunities that are hidden within every challenge.

Another important benefit of positive thinking is that it helps us to build confidence and self-esteem. When we believe in ourselves and our abilities, we are more likely to take bold action and to achieve our goals. Positive thinking helps us to see ourselves as capable and competent, and this in turn helps us to build the courage we need to take risks and pursue our dreams.

But perhaps the most powerful benefit of positive thinking is that it helps us to create the life we want. When we focus on positive thoughts, we become a magnet for positive energy and we attract the people, opportunities, and resources we need to achieve our goals. This is because positive thinking helps us to align our thoughts, words, and actions with our deepest desires and aspirations.

In conclusion, the power of positive thinking is truly remarkable and can help you to achieve your goals and dreams. By focusing on positive thoughts, you can shift your perspective, build resilience, boost your confidence, and create the life you want. Remember, your thoughts have the power to shape your reality, so choose them wisely.

Chapter Sixteen: The Importance of Self-Awareness: Understanding Your Needs and Emotions

Discovering Your Authentic Self

Discovering your authentic self is not just about finding who you are, it's about uncovering the true essence of your being and living in alignment with your core values and beliefs. It's about letting go of the societal norms and expectations that have been imposed upon you, and embracing your unique individuality.

One of the first steps in discovering your authentic self is to question everything you've been taught and everything you believe. Take a step back and examine your beliefs, values and habits. Are they truly your own, or have they been passed down to you by others? Once you've identified the beliefs and values that are truly yours, you can start to build a life that is in alignment with them.

Another important aspect of discovering your authentic self is to learn to trust your intuition. Our intuition is a powerful tool that can guide us towards our true selves. It's important to listen to that inner voice, even when it goes against the grain of what society deems as "normal" or "acceptable."

Another key aspect of discovering your authentic self is to take the time to get to know yourself. This means taking the time to reflect on your thoughts, feelings, and emotions. It's important to understand your own emotional landscape and to learn how to navigate it. This can be done through journaling, meditation, therapy or other introspective practices.

One of the most powerful ways to discover your authentic self is through self-care. Taking care of your physical, emotional and spiritual needs is vital to your overall well-being and will help you to connect with your true self. This can include things like exercise, healthy eating, and regular self-reflection.

One practical example of discovering your authentic self is the story of a man named John. John had always been told that he should become a lawyer, just like his father and grandfather before him. However, deep down, John had a passion for art and design. He ignored his intuition and followed in his family's footsteps, becoming a lawyer. But he was unfulfilled and found himself constantly daydreaming about pursuing a career in art and design. Eventually, John listened to his intuition and made the difficult decision to leave his successful law practice to pursue his true passion in art and design. Today, John is a renowned artist and designer, living a life true to his authentic self.

Another example is a woman named Sarah, who always felt like she didn't fit in with her friends and family. She never felt like she belonged, and she couldn't understand why. She took the time to get to know herself better, and through journaling and therapy, she realized that she was a deeply spiritual person. She had always been interested in different spiritual practices, but she had never taken the time to explore them further. Sarah began to incorporate different spiritual practices into her life and started to feel a sense of belonging and fulfillment that she had never felt before.

In conclusion, discovering your authentic self is not just about finding yourself, it's about becoming the person you were meant to be. It's about embracing your unique individuality, trusting your intuition, understanding your own emotional landscape, and taking care of your physical, emotional and spiritual needs. It's about living in alignment with your core values and beliefs, and living a life true to yourself. Remember, as the ancient Greek philosopher Epictetus said, "Know, first, who you are, and then adorn yourself accordingly."

The Power of Self-Reflection

Self-reflection is a powerful tool that can help us to better understand ourselves and our actions, and to make positive changes in our lives. Yet, many people overlook the importance of this practice, and fail to take the time to truly reflect on their thoughts, feelings, and behaviors.

At its core, self-reflection is about taking a step back and examining our own thoughts and actions, without judgment. It allows us to gain insight into our own motivations, and to understand the underlying reasons for our actions. This process can be difficult and uncomfortable, but it is essential for personal growth and self-improvement.

One of the key benefits of self-reflection is that it helps us to identify and challenge negative thought patterns and beliefs. We all have limiting beliefs that hold us back in life, whether it is a belief that we are not good enough, or that we will never achieve our goals. Through self-reflection, we can begin to identify these limiting beliefs, and to challenge and replace them with more positive and empowering thoughts.

Another powerful aspect of self-reflection is that it helps us to understand the impact of our actions on others. We often get caught up in our own perspectives and fail to consider the perspectives of others. By taking the time to reflect on our interactions with others, we can gain a deeper understanding of how our actions affect those around us, and make changes as needed.

One practical example of the power of self-reflection is a woman named Sarah, who had always struggled with feelings of insecurity and low self-esteem. She found that she often put herself down and had a hard time accepting compliments. Through self-reflection, Sarah was able to identify the root cause of her insecurity: a past relationship where she was constantly belittled and made to feel worthless by her partner. By confronting this issue and working through the hurt and trauma from that relationship, Sarah was able to let go of those negative thought patterns and build a healthier and more positive sense of self.

Another example is a man named John, who had a tendency to be short-tempered and easily irritated. He often found himself snapping at colleagues and loved ones, causing strain in his relationships. Through self-reflection, John realized that he was under a lot of stress and pressure in his job, and that his short temper was a result of pent up frustration. He started practicing mindfulness and stress-management techniques, which helped him to be more aware of his emotions and to respond in a more measured and calm way.

Self-reflection can also be used to set and achieve goals. By taking the time to reflect on what we truly want in life, we can identify our priorities and set clear, achievable goals. It can also help us to create a plan of action, and to stay motivated as we work towards achieving our goals.

One of the greatest benefits of self-reflection is that it allows us to connect with our true selves. In today's fast-paced world, it is all too easy to get caught up in the hustle and bustle of daily life, and to lose sight of what truly matters to us. By taking the time to reflect on our thoughts, feelings, and actions, we can gain a deeper understanding of our own wants and needs, and work towards living a more authentic and fulfilling life.

In conclusion, self-reflection is an incredibly powerful tool that can help us to better understand ourselves, overcome negative thought patterns, improve our relationships, and achieve our goals. It is a process that may be difficult and uncomfortable, but it is essential for personal growth and self-improvement. As the ancient Greek philosopher, Socrates, once said, "The unexamined life

Navigating Emotions: A Guide to Understanding Your Needs

Navigating emotions can be a difficult and confusing task, but understanding your needs is the key to unlocking a more fulfilling and balanced life. Emotions are often seen as something to be avoided or repressed, but they are actually an important part of our human experience. They help us to understand and connect with ourselves and others, and provide valuable insight into our needs and desires.

The first step in understanding your needs is to become aware of your emotions. This means paying attention to how you feel and what triggers those feelings. It's important to remember that emotions are not good or bad, they simply are. They are a natural response to our environment and experiences.

Once you become aware of your emotions, it's important to identify the underlying needs that are driving them. For example, if you feel angry, it may be because you feel disrespected or unsupported. If you feel anxious, it may be because you feel uncertain or out of control. By identifying the underlying needs, you can better understand what actions need to be taken to address them.

It's also important to remember that our emotions are often connected to one another. For example, anger can often be linked to feelings of hurt or sadness. This means that by addressing one emotion, you may also be addressing others.

It's important to understand that emotions are not something that can be controlled, but they can be managed. One way to do this is through the use of mindfulness techniques, such as meditation or journaling. These practices can help you to become more aware of your emotions and to understand the underlying needs that are driving them.

Another way to manage emotions is through self-care. This means taking care of your physical, emotional, and mental well-being. This can include things like getting enough sleep, eating well, and engaging in activities that bring you joy. By taking care of yourself, you can better manage your emotions and address the underlying needs that are driving them.

It's also important to understand that emotions are not something that can be controlled, but they can be managed. One way to do this is through the use of mindfulness techniques, such as meditation or journaling. These practices can help you to become more aware of your emotions and to understand the underlying needs that are driving them.

Another way to manage emotions is through self -care. This means taking care of your physical, emotional, and mental well-being. This can include things like getting enough sleep, eating well, and engaging in activities that bring you joy. By taking care of yourself, you can better manage your emotions and address the underlying needs that are driving them.

It is also important to have a support system in place. This can include friends, family, or a therapist. They can provide a safe space for you to talk about your emotions and can offer valuable perspective and advice.

It is also important to practice self-compassion. This means being kind and understanding towards yourself, instead of being self-critical or judgmental. Self-compassion can help to reduce stress and anxiety and increase feelings of well-being.

In addition, it is important to learn to set boundaries, especially when it comes to dealing with toxic people or situations. By setting boundaries, you can better protect yourself and your emotional well-being.

Finally, it is important to remember that emotions are not permanent. They come and go, and they will change as you change. By understanding your needs, managing your emotions, and taking care of yourself, you can navigate your emotions with greater ease and find a sense of balance and fulfillment in your life.

In conclusion, emotions are an essential part of our human experience and understanding our needs is the key to unlocking a more fulfilling and balanced life. By becoming aware of our emotions, identifying the underlying needs that drive them, managing them through mindfulness techniques and self-care, having a support system and practicing self-compassion, setting boundaries and remembering that emotions are not permanent, we can navigate our emotions with greater ease and find a sense of balance and fulfillment in our life.

Building Emotional Intelligence: The Key to Self-Awareness

Emotional intelligence (EI) is the ability to understand and manage our own emotions, as well as the emotions of others. It is a crucial component of self-awareness, which is the foundation of personal development and growth. Building emotional intelligence is the key to unlocking our full potential and living a more fulfilled and meaningful life.

The first step in building emotional intelligence is understanding our emotions. Many of us have been taught to suppress or ignore our emotions, which can lead to a disconnection from ourselves. To build emotional intelligence, we must learn to recognize and acknowledge our emotions, rather than pushing them away. This can be done through mindfulness and self-reflection.

Mindfulness is the practice of being present in the moment and paying attention to our thoughts and feelings without judgment. When we are mindful, we are able to observe our emotions without becoming overwhelmed by them. This allows us to gain a deeper understanding of our emotions and how they influence our behavior.

Self-reflection is another important aspect of understanding our emotions. By taking time to reflect on our emotions, we can gain insight into the underlying causes of our feelings and how they relate to our thoughts and actions. This can help us to become more self-aware and better equipped to manage our emotions.

The second step in building emotional intelligence is managing our emotions. This means learning to regulate our emotions and respond to them in a constructive way. One way to do this is through emotional regulation techniques such as deep breathing, progressive muscle relaxation, and visualization.

Deep breathing is a simple yet powerful technique for managing emotions. When we breathe deeply, we activate the parasympathetic nervous system, which helps to calm our body and mind. This can help to reduce feelings of anxiety and stress, and increase feelings of relaxation and peace.

Progressive muscle relaxation is another technique that can help to reduce tension and stress. This involves tensing and then relaxing each muscle group in the body, starting with the feet and working up to the head. As we relax each muscle group, we release the tension and stress that has been stored in that area of the body.

Visualization is a powerful tool for managing emotions. By visualizing a calm and peaceful scene, we can create a sense of calm and relaxation within ourselves. This can help to reduce feelings of stress and anxiety and increase feelings of positivity and well-being. It can be helpful to choose a visualization that is specific and meaningful to you, such as a peaceful beach or a peaceful forest. It can also be helpful to incorporate the five senses into your visualization, such as the sound of waves or the smell of pine trees.

Another technique for managing emotions is through the use of positive affirmations. Positive affirmations are statements that you repeat to yourself to change your mindset and beliefs. These statements can help to shift your focus from negative emotions to positive emotions, and promote feelings of self-worth and confidence.

The third step in building emotional intelligence is empathy, the ability to understand and share the feelings of others. Empathy is important because it allows us to connect with others on a deeper level and to understand their perspective. It also helps to promote compassion and understanding, which can lead to more positive relationships.

One way to practice empathy is through active listening. This means truly listening to what the other person is saying and trying to understand their perspective. It can also be helpful to put yourself in their shoes and imagine how you would feel if you were in their situation.

Another way to practice empathy is through expressing gratitude. When we take the time to appreciate and acknowledge the positive aspects of our relationships, it can help to build deeper connections and understanding with others.

Lastly, to build emotional intelligence, we need to practice self-compassion. Self-compassion is the ability to be kind and understanding towards ourselves, especially when we make mistakes or fail. It is important to remember that we are all human and we all make mistakes. By practicing self-compassion, we can develop more resilience, and learn to bounce back more quickly from setbacks.

In conclusion, building emotional intelligence is the key to self-awareness. By understanding our emotions, managing them and empathizing with others, we can lead a more fulfilling and meaningful life. Remember to practice mindfulness, self-reflection, visualization, positive affirmations, active listening, gratitude and self-compassion. By implementing these practical examples in your daily routine, you will be able to improve your emotional intelligence, and ultimately live a happier and more harmonious life.

The Link Between Self-Awareness and Mental Health

Self-awareness is defined as the ability to recognize and understand one's own emotions, thoughts, and behavior. It is a crucial aspect of mental health as it allows individuals to understand and regulate their emotions, make better decisions, and form healthier relationships. However, not all individuals possess the same level of self-awareness, and for some, it may be a journey to achieve it.

Famous author and psychoanalyst Carl Jung once said, "Knowing your own darkness is the best method for dealing with the darknesses of other people." This quote highlights the importance of self-awareness in understanding one's own thoughts and emotions, and how it can aid in understanding and interacting with others.

Self-awareness is closely linked to emotional intelligence, which is the ability to identify, understand, and manage one's own emotions and the emotions of others. When individuals possess a high level of emotional intelligence, they are better equipped to handle challenging situations and maintain positive relationships. In his book "Emotional Intelligence," author Daniel Goleman states, "Self-awareness is the foundation of emotional intelligence."

Practical examples of the link between self-awareness and mental health can be seen in various forms of therapy, such as cognitive-behavioral therapy (CBT) and mindfulness-based therapy. CBT focuses on identifying and changing negative thought patterns that can lead to mental health issues, such as depression and anxiety. Mindfulness-based therapy, on the other hand, emphasizes being present in the moment and observing one's thoughts and emotions without judgment. Both of these therapies require a high level of self-awareness in order to be effective.

Famous author and philosopher Friedrich Nietzsche once wrote, "He who has a why to live for can bear almost any how." This quote highlights the importance of having a sense of purpose and meaning in one's life, which can be achieved through self-awareness. When individuals understand their values, beliefs, and goals, they are better equipped to find purpose and fulfillment in their lives.

Self-awareness also plays a crucial role in the development of healthy relationships. Author and relationship expert John Gottman states, "Self-awareness is the ability to see oneself as one really is and to accept that reality." When individuals possess a high level of self-awareness, they are better equipped to understand their own needs and communicate them effectively to their partners, leading to healthier and more fulfilling relationships. They are also better able to empathize with their partners and understand their perspective, which can lead to more effective conflict resolution.

Self-awareness is also important in the workplace, as it allows individuals to understand how their behavior and actions may affect others. Famous author and management expert Peter Drucker once said, "The most important thing in communication is hearing what isn't being said." When individuals possess a high level of self-awareness, they are better able to pick up on subtle cues and understand the unspoken thoughts and emotions of their colleagues, leading to more effective communication and collaboration.

In conclusion, self-awareness is a crucial aspect of mental health as it allows individuals to understand and regulate their emotions, make better decisions, and form healthier relationships. It is a journey that requires ongoing reflection and introspection, but the benefits of achieving a high level of self-awareness are well worth the effort. As famous author and poet Ralph Waldo Emerson once said, "The eye is the first circle; the horizon which it forms is the second; and throughout nature this primary figure is repeated without end." Self-awareness is the first step in understanding ourselves and the world around us.

The Impact of Social Media on Self-Awareness

Social media has revolutionized the way we communicate and interact with each other. It has also had a profound impact on our self-awareness. The constant stream of information and constant pressure to present a curated version of ourselves online can have both positive and negative effects on our self-awareness.

On the one hand, social media can help us to better understand and express ourselves. Platforms like Instagram and TikTok allow us to share our interests and passions with a global audience, giving us a sense of validation and belonging. Social media can also be a powerful tool for personal growth and self-discovery. The ability to connect with like-minded individuals and access a wealth of information can help us to expand our perspectives and develop new skills.

However, social media can also be detrimental to our self-awareness. The pressure to present a perfect image online can lead to feelings of inadequacy and self-doubt. We may compare ourselves to the curated versions of others, creating unrealistic expectations and a distorted sense of reality. Social media can also foster a culture of narcissism and self-obsession, leading us to prioritize external validation over genuine self-reflection.

The famous author George Orwell in his book "1984" had a similar opinion on the impact of technology on self-awareness. He wrote, "If you want to keep a secret, you must also hide it from yourself." The idea is that the constant surveillance and lack of privacy in the novel's society leads to a self-censorship, where individuals are not even aware of their own thoughts and feelings. This is a stark reminder of how technology can inhibit self-awareness and personal freedom.

On the other hand, Haruki Murakami in his book "1Q84" explored the idea of how technology can open new worlds of self-discovery. He wrote, "Once you've read a book and it becomes part of your being, you'll never be the same again." This quote highlights how technology, specifically books in this case, can open new perspectives and ways of understanding ourselves.

In practical terms, to maintain a healthy level of self-awareness while using social media, it is important to set boundaries and engage in self-reflection. It is essential to be mindful of the amount of time we spend on social media, and to take regular breaks from the constant stream of information. This can help us to avoid feelings of overwhelm and disconnect from the pressure to present a curated version of ourselves online.

It's also important to be mindful of the content we consume on social media. Following accounts that align with our values and interests can help us to expand our perspectives and develop a deeper understanding of ourselves. On the other hand, constantly comparing ourselves to others can lead to feelings of inadequacy and self-doubt.

Additionally, it's crucial to be mindful of the information we share on social media. It can be tempting to present an idealized version of ourselves online, but it's important to remember that social media is not always an accurate reflection of reality. By being honest and authentic in our online interactions, we can develop a more accurate and nuanced understanding of ourselves.

In conclusion, social media can have both positive and negative effects on our self-awareness. However, by setting boundaries, engaging in self-reflection and being mindful of the content we consume and share, we can use social media as a tool for personal growth and self-discovery. As famous author J.D. Salinger once wrote, "The mark of the immature man is that he wants to die nobly for a cause, while the mark of the mature man is that he wants to live humbly for one." This quote highlights the importance of being authentic and true to oneself, something that can be achieved by being aware of the impact of social media on self-awareness.

Self-Awareness in the Workplace: The Importance of Self-Reflection

Self-awareness in the workplace is a critical aspect of personal and professional growth. It involves the ability to understand one's own emotions, thoughts, and actions and how they impact oneself and others. Self-awareness is essential for effective communication, building and maintaining relationships, and making sound decisions. The importance of self-reflection in achieving self-awareness cannot be overstated.

Self-reflection is the process of introspection, where an individual takes the time to examine their thoughts, feelings, and actions. It is a vital tool for gaining insight into one's own behavior and understanding how it affects others. Self-reflection allows individuals to identify areas of improvement, set goals, and make necessary changes to achieve their desired outcomes.

In the workplace, self-awareness and self-reflection are essential for effective leadership and teamwork. A leader who is self-aware is better equipped to understand the needs and perspectives of their team members and make decisions that align with the organization's objectives. They are also more likely to foster a positive and productive work environment.

Self-reflection is also essential for effective communication. By understanding one's own emotions and perspective, individuals can better understand how to express themselves and respond to the needs of others. As the renowned author and speaker Brené Brown said, "clear is kind. Unclear is unkind." Self-awareness allows individuals to communicate clearly and effectively, reducing misunderstandings and conflicts.

Effective problem-solving also requires self-awareness and self-reflection. When faced with a problem, individuals who are self-aware are better equipped to consider multiple perspectives and find creative solutions. As the fictional detective Sherlock Holmes famously said, "it is a capital mistake to theorize before one has data." Self-awareness allows individuals to gather all necessary information before making decisions.

Self-awareness and self-reflection are also essential for personal growth and development. As the writer and poet Maya Angelou said, "I did then what I knew how to do. Now that I know better, I do better." Self-reflection allows individuals to identify areas of improvement and set goals to achieve them.

In conclusion, self-awareness in the workplace is a crucial aspect of personal and professional growth. Self-reflection is a vital tool for achieving self-awareness, as it allows individuals to understand their thoughts, feelings, and actions and how they impact themselves and others. By practicing self-reflection, individuals can identify areas of improvement, set goals, and make necessary changes to achieve their desired outcomes. Self-awareness and self-reflection are essential for effective leadership, teamwork, communication, problem-solving, and personal growth and development. It enables individuals to communicate clearly, foster positive work environment, find creative solutions, and continuously improve themselves.

It is important to note that self-reflection is not a one-time exercise, it is a continuous process that requires consistency and commitment. Employers should also encourage and provide resources for their employees to practice self-awareness and self-reflection. This can be achieved through regular performance evaluations, team-building exercises, and personal development programs. By fostering a culture of self-awareness and self-reflection in the workplace, individuals and organizations can achieve greater success and fulfillment.

The Role of Self-Awareness in Building Strong Relationships

Self-awareness is the foundation upon which all successful relationships are built. When we are self-aware, we are able to understand our own thoughts, feelings, and actions, as well as how they impact those around us. This understanding allows us to navigate our relationships with greater ease and intimacy, and to build stronger, more meaningful connections with others.

One of the most important aspects of self-awareness is the ability to understand and manage our own emotions. As the famous author Jane Austen wrote in her novel "Sense and Sensibility," "The more I know of the world, the more I am convinced that I shall never see a man whom I can really love." This sentiment highlights the importance of understanding our own emotional needs and desires in order to build healthy relationships. When we are able to identify and manage our own emotions, we are better equipped to communicate effectively with others and to understand their perspectives.

Another key aspect of self-awareness is the ability to understand and accept our own limitations and strengths. As the renowned author George Orwell wrote in his novel "Animal Farm," "All animals are equal, but some animals are more equal than others." This quote highlights the importance of understanding and accepting our own limitations, while also recognizing and valuing the strengths of others. By doing so, we are able to build stronger, more equal relationships based on mutual understanding and respect.

In addition to understanding and managing our own emotions and limitations, self-awareness also involves the ability to understand and accept the emotions and limitations of others. As the famous author J.D. Salinger wrote in his novel "The Catcher in the Rye," "I'm quite illiterate, but I read a lot." This quote highlights the importance of being open to the perspectives and experiences of others, even if they are different from our own. By understanding and accepting the emotions and limitations of others, we are able to build stronger, more empathetic relationships based on mutual understanding and compassion.

Practical examples of how self-awareness can be applied in building strong relationships can be found in everyday life. For example, imagine a couple who is having a disagreement about household chores. If one partner is self-aware, they will be able to understand and manage their own emotions, and to communicate effectively with their partner. They might say something like, "I understand that I have been feeling overwhelmed with my workload at the office and have not been able to contribute as much to the household chores as I would like. Can we discuss ways in which we can both take on more responsibility and find a solution that works for both of us?" This approach shows self-awareness by acknowledging one's own emotions and limitations, and by being open to finding a mutually beneficial solution.

Another practical example of self-awareness in building strong relationships can be found in friendships. Imagine a friend who has been going through a tough time and is struggling with their mental health. If you are self-aware, you will be able to understand and accept your friend's emotions and limitations, and offer support in a way that is appropriate and non-judgmental. You might say something like, "I understand that you have been going through a tough time and I want to support you. Can I help by listening, or is there something else you need?" This approach shows self-awareness by being empathetic and understanding towards your friend's needs.

In conclusion, self-awareness is a crucial ingredient for building strong relationships. It allows us to understand and manage our own emotions, limitations, and strengths, as well as those of others. By being self-aware, we are better equipped to navigate our relationships with ease and intimacy, and to build stronger, more meaningful connections with others. As the famous author Maya Angelou once wrote, "I've learned that people will forget what you said, people will forget what you did, but people will never forget how you made them feel." By being self-aware, we can make others feel understood, accepted, and valued, ultimately leading to strong and healthy relationships.

The Connection Between Self-Awareness and Personal Growth

Self-awareness is the keystone of personal growth, and understanding the connection between the two is essential for anyone looking to improve themselves and live a more fulfilling life.

Self-awareness is the ability to recognize and understand one's own thoughts, emotions, and behaviors, and how they affect oneself and others. Personal growth, on the other hand, is the continuous process of developing oneself, both mentally and emotionally.

One practical example of the connection between self-awareness and personal growth can be seen in the character development of Holden Caulfield in J.D. Salinger's "The Catcher in the Rye." Throughout the novel, Holden struggles with self-awareness, often acting impulsively and failing to understand the consequences of his actions. However, as the novel progresses, Holden begins to gain a better understanding of himself and his behavior. He starts to realize the impact his actions have on those around him, and he begins to make changes in his life. By the end of the novel, Holden has grown significantly, both as a person and as a character. This example illustrates how self-awareness is a crucial first step in personal growth, as it allows one to understand their own behavior and make conscious choices about how to change it.

Another practical example of the connection between self-awareness and personal growth can be seen in the character development of Ebenezer Scrooge in Charles Dickens's "A Christmas Carol." At the beginning of the story, Scrooge is a miserly and uncaring man, completely lacking in self-awareness. However, through a series of ghostly encounters, Scrooge begins to gain insight into his own behavior and how it affects those around him. He starts to understand the importance of kindness and compassion, and he begins to make changes in his life. By the end of the story, Scrooge has grown significantly, both as a person and as a character. This example illustrates how self-awareness can lead to a change in perspective, which can in turn lead to personal growth.

As renowned author Brené Brown puts it, "Self-awareness is the capacity for introspection and the ability to recognize oneself as an individual separate from the environment and other individuals." In other words, self-awareness is the ability to step back and observe oneself objectively. It is the first step in personal growth because it allows one to understand their own behavior and thought patterns, and to recognize areas in which they need to improve. Without self-awareness, it is impossible to make meaningful changes in one's life.

Self-awareness also helps in personal growth by allowing one to take responsibility for their actions and to understand the impact they have on others. As renowned author and philosopher, Eckhart Tolle said, "Realize deeply that the present moment is all you have. Make the NOW the primary focus of your life." When we are self-aware, we are more present in the moment and able to recognize when we are acting in ways that are not in line with our values or goals. This allows us to make conscious choices about how we want to behave in the future.

Furthermore, self-awareness also helps in personal growth by allowing one to identify their strengths and weaknesses and to focus on developing their strengths. As renowned author, Stephen Covey, said, "The greatest need of a human being is to see oneself as capable, significant, to be worthy of respect." When we are self-aware, we can identify our strengths and use them to achieve our goals. We can also recognize our weaknesses and work on improving them.

In conclusion, self-awareness and personal growth are closely connected, self-awareness is the foundation upon which personal growth is built. Without self-awareness, it is impossible to make meaningful changes in one's life. As we strive for personal growth, let us remember to continually work on developing our self-awareness, for it is through self-awareness that we can truly understand ourselves and make conscious choices about how to live our lives.

Chapter Seventeen: The Lone Wolf and Leadership: Developing Your Leadership Skills

The myth of the "lone wolf" leader

The concept of the "lone wolf" leader, a solitary figure who rises to power through their own determination and ingenuity, is a pervasive myth in both literature and real-world politics. This archetype is often celebrated for their independence and self-sufficiency, but in reality, true leadership is a collaborative effort that requires the support and input of a team.

In Chinese literature, the famous novel "Romance of the Three Kingdoms" written by Luo Guanzhong, depicts the characters of Liu Bei, Cao Cao, and Sun Jian as "lone wolf" leaders. Each of them is portrayed as a powerful and charismatic figure who is able to rally support and defeat their enemies through their own strength and determination. However, as the novel progresses, it becomes clear that the true power of these leaders comes not from their individual abilities, but from the loyal and dedicated teams they have built around them. Liu Bei's success is largely due to the support of his sworn brothers Guan Yu and Zhang Fei, while Cao Cao's victories are made possible by the strategic advice of his advisors and the bravery of his soldiers.

Similarly, in Italian literature, the novel "The Prince" written by Niccolò Machiavelli, presents the idea of the "lone wolf" leader as a ruler who must be willing to do whatever is necessary to maintain power, even if it means going against traditional moral codes. However, the novel also emphasizes the importance of building and maintaining alliances and support networks in order to effectively rule. Machiavelli writes, "One who becomes a Prince through the favor of the people should always keep on good terms with them; which it is easy for him to do since all men are naturally alike in wishing to get themselves forward, and he has nothing to fear from them so long as he does not stand in their way."

In real-world politics, the myth of the "lone wolf" leader can be seen in leaders who prioritize personal ambition over collaboration and teamwork. Such leaders may believe that they alone have the answers to complex problems and refuse to listen to the input and advice of others. However, in practice, this kind of leadership is often ineffective and can even be detrimental to the organization or country they are leading.

One example of this is the leadership style of former Italian Prime Minister Silvio Berlusconi, who was known for his brash and controversial leadership style. Berlusconi was often criticized for making decisions without consulting his advisors or party members, and for prioritizing his own personal interests over the needs of the country. This ultimately led to his government being plagued by scandals and political turmoil, and his administration was eventually forced to resign.

Another example is the leadership style of former Chinese leader Mao Zedong, who is known for his authoritarian leadership and the cultural revolution. Mao's leadership style was characterized by a lack of consultation with other leaders, and his decisions were often made without the input of experts or other government officials. This led to a number of major policy failures and human rights abuses, and it ultimately resulted in widespread suffering and economic stagnation for the Chinese people.

In contrast, successful leaders such as Nelson Mandela, Mahatma Gandhi and Angela Merkel, have shown that true leadership is a collaborative effort that requires the support and input of a team. Mandela, for example, was able to unite a divided South Africa through his ability to bring different factions together and build a sense of shared purpose. Similarly, Gandhi's non-violent leadership style inspired millions of Indians to join the freedom movement and helped India to gain independence from British colonial rule. Angela Merkel as well has been able to lead Germany through her ability to build coalitions and work with other leaders to achieve common goals.

In conclusion, the myth of the "lone wolf" leader is a harmful and outdated concept that is not reflective of the realities of leadership. True leadership is a collaborative effort that requires the support and input of a team. It is important to recognize the importance of building and maintaining alliances and support networks in order to effectively lead. As Machiavelli wrote "A Prince who is not wise himself will never take good advice."

The importance of self-awareness in leadership

Self-awareness is the ability to understand one's own emotions, thoughts, and behaviors and how they impact others. In leadership, self-awareness is crucial in understanding how one's actions and decisions affect not only oneself but also the team or organization. Without self-awareness, a leader may make decisions that are detrimental to the team and the overall success of the organization.

One of the most important aspects of self-awareness in leadership is the ability to understand and manage one's emotions. As the famous Russian author Fyodor Dostoevsky writes in his novel "Crime and Punishment," "Above all, don't lie to yourself. The man who lies to himself and listens to his own lie comes to a point that he cannot distinguish the truth within him, or around him, and so loses all respect for himself and for others." A leader who is not self-aware may be prone to making decisions based on their emotions rather than logical reasoning, which can have negative consequences for the team.

Another important aspect of self-awareness in leadership is the ability to understand one's own strengths and weaknesses. A leader who is not self-aware may overestimate their abilities and take on tasks that they are not prepared for, leading to poor performance and disappointment. The famous Turkish author Orhan Pamuk writes in his novel "My Name is Red," "To be a good artist, you have to know yourself, to understand your own weaknesses and strengths." A leader who is self-aware can use this understanding to delegate tasks to others who are better suited for them and to focus on tasks that they excel at.

Self-awareness also involves understanding how one's actions and decisions affect others. A leader who is not self-aware may make decisions that are beneficial to themselves but detrimental to the team. As the Russian author Leo Tolstoy writes in his novel "War and Peace," "A man is like a fraction whose numerator is what he is and whose denominator is what he thinks of himself. The larger the denominator, the smaller the fraction." A leader who is self-aware can understand how their actions and decisions may be perceived by others and make adjustments accordingly.

One practical way to improve self-awareness in leadership is through regular self-reflection. This can include journaling, meditating, or seeking feedback from team members. By regularly taking the time to reflect on one's actions and decisions, a leader can gain a better understanding of how they are perceived by others and identify areas for improvement. Additionally, seeking feedback from team members can provide valuable insight into how a leader's actions are impacting the team and provide specific examples of areas that need improvement.

Another practical way to improve self-awareness in leadership is by learning from others. This can be done by reading books or articles on leadership, attending workshops or conferences, or seeking mentorship from experienced leaders. By learning from others, a leader can gain a better understanding of different leadership styles and techniques and apply them to their own leadership approach.

Additionally, a leader can improve self-awareness by being open to constructive criticism and learning from mistakes. As the Turkish author Elif Shafak writes in her novel "The Bastard of Istanbul," "We learn from failure, not from success!" A leader who is open to constructive criticism and willing to learn from their mistakes is more likely to improve their self-awareness and become a more effective leader.

In conclusion, self-awareness is a vital aspect of leadership. It enables a leader to understand and manage their emotions, understand their strengths and weaknesses, and understand how their actions affect others. Through regular self-reflection, seeking feedback, learning from others, being open to constructive criticism, and learning from mistakes, a leader can improve their self-awareness and become a more effective leader.

Building a strong personal brand as a leader

Building a strong personal brand as a leader is crucial for success in today's competitive business landscape. A personal brand is the unique combination of skills, values, and personality that sets you apart from others and establishes your credibility and reputation as a leader. Developing a strong personal brand can help you to build trust and credibility with your team, clients, and stakeholders, and ultimately, achieve your goals and aspirations.

One key aspect of building a strong personal brand as a leader is authenticity. As the fictional Russian author Leo Tolstoy once wrote, "Everyone thinks of changing the world, but no one thinks of changing himself." True leaders understand that in order to be effective, they must first be true to themselves. They must be authentic in their actions, words, and values, and they must be willing to take risks and be vulnerable. Authenticity is the foundation upon which trust and credibility are built, and it is essential for establishing a strong personal brand.

Another essential aspect of building a strong personal brand as a leader is the ability to communicate effectively. As the fictional Turkish author Orhan Pamuk once wrote, "The role of a writer is not to say what we can all say, but what we are unable to say." Effective leaders understand the importance of clear and compelling communication, and they are able to convey their message in a way that is both relatable and inspiring. They are able to connect with their audience on a deep level, and they are able to use their words to influence and inspire others.

In addition to authenticity and effective communication, building a strong personal brand as a leader also requires a deep understanding of one's own strengths and weaknesses. As the fictional Russian author Fyodor Dostoevsky wrote, "Above all, don't lie to yourself. The man who lies to himself and listens to his own lie comes to a point that he cannot distinguish the truth within him, or around him, and so loses all respect for himself and for others." Leaders who have a deep understanding of their own strengths and weaknesses are able to make better decisions, lead more effectively, and build stronger relationships.

Practical examples of building a strong personal brand can be seen in the leaders who stand out in the industry, such as Oprah Winfrey, Elon Musk, and Richard Branson. Oprah Winfrey, for example, is known for her authenticity and ability to connect with her audience on a personal level. She has built a strong personal brand as a leader by being true to herself and her values, and by consistently delivering inspiring and relatable content.

Elon Musk, on the other hand, is known for his ability to think outside the box and take risks. He has built a strong personal brand as a leader by consistently pushing the boundaries of what is possible and by challenging the status quo. He is also known for being transparent with his communication, and for being an inspiring leader to his team and stakeholders.

Richard Branson is another example of a leader with a strong personal brand. He is known for his ability to inspire and lead others, and for his ability to think big and take bold risks. He has built a strong personal brand by consistently delivering on his promises and by being an authentic and relatable leader.

In conclusion, building a strong personal brand as a leader requires authenticity, effective communication, and a deep understanding of one's own strengths and weaknesses. It's important to be true to oneself and one's values, to be able to connect and communicate with others, and to be aware of one's own limitations. Practical examples of leaders who have successfully built a strong personal brand include Oprah Winfrey, Elon Musk, and Richard

Branson, however, the key is to find your own unique way of building your personal brand. As Leo Tolstoy once wrote, "The two most powerful warriors are patience and time." Building a personal brand takes time, patience and consistency, but when you do it, the result will be worth it.

Developing emotional intelligence in leadership

Emotional intelligence is a critical component of effective leadership. It is the ability to recognize, understand and manage one's own emotions, as well as the emotions of others. This skill set allows leaders to create a positive and productive work environment, build strong relationships, and make better decisions. In this article, we will explore the importance of emotional intelligence in leadership and provide practical examples and quotes from renowned fictional Russian and Turkish authors to illustrate the concepts discussed.

One of the key benefits of emotional intelligence in leadership is the ability to effectively communicate with and motivate others. As the famous Russian author, Fyodor Dostoevsky, wrote in his classic novel, Crime and Punishment, "The greatest happiness is to know the source of unhappiness." A leader who is emotionally intelligent is able to identify and understand the emotions of their team members, and use this understanding to create a positive work environment. They are able to empathize with their team members, and provide the support and guidance they need to be successful. In doing so, they create a culture of trust and respect, which leads to increased motivation and productivity.

Another important aspect of emotional intelligence in leadership is the ability to make effective decisions. As the Turkish author Orhan Pamuk wrote in his novel, Snow, "To understand a person's life, you have to understand their fears." A leader who is emotionally intelligent is able to recognize and understand their own emotions and biases, which allows them to make more objective and rational decisions. They are able to separate their personal feelings from the task at hand, and make decisions based on what is best for the organization and its goals. In doing so, they are able to lead their team to success and achieve their objectives.

Emotional intelligence also plays a crucial role in building and maintaining strong relationships. As Dostoevsky wrote in his novel, The Brothers Karamazov, "Love all God's creation, both the whole of it and every grain of sand. Love every leaf, every ray of God's light. Love the animals, love the plants, love everything." A leader who is emotionally intelligent is able to connect with others on a deeper level, which creates a sense of trust and respect. They are able to understand and appreciate the perspectives of others, which allows them to build strong relationships and create a sense of unity within the organization.

The importance of clear communication in leadership

Clear communication is a critical aspect of leadership. It is essential for leaders to be able to effectively convey their vision, goals, and expectations to their team. Clear communication not only ensures that everyone is on the same page, but it also helps to foster a sense of trust and understanding within the team.

French author, Antoine de Saint-Exupéry once said, "If you want to build a ship, don't drum up people to collect wood and don't assign them tasks and work, but rather teach them to long for the endless immensity of the sea." This quote illustrates the importance of clear communication in leadership. A leader must be able to clearly communicate their vision and inspire their team to work towards a common goal.

One practical example of clear communication in leadership is through the use of clear and concise language. A leader should avoid using jargon or complex language that may be confusing to their team. Instead, they should use simple and straightforward language that is easily understood by everyone. This helps to ensure that everyone is on the same page and working towards the same goal.

Another example of clear communication in leadership is through active listening. A leader should actively listen to their team and be open to feedback and suggestions. This helps to create a culture of open communication and collaboration within the team. French author, Albert Camus, once said, "The most important thing is to listen." This quote emphasizes the importance of active listening in leadership. A leader should listen to their team and take their feedback and suggestions into consideration when making decisions.

Clear communication also involves being transparent and honest with your team. French author, Victor Hugo, once said, "The greatest happiness of life is the conviction that we are loved; loved for ourselves, or rather, loved in spite of ourselves." A leader should be transparent and honest with their team, even when delivering difficult news. This helps to build trust and understanding within the team.

In conclusion, clear communication is a critical aspect of leadership. It is essential for leaders to be able to effectively convey their vision, goals, and expectations to their team. Clear communication helps to foster a sense of trust and understanding within the team and ensures that everyone is working towards the same goal. Practical examples of clear communication in leadership include the use of clear and concise language, active listening, and transparency and honesty. As French author, Antoine de Saint-Exupéry, once said, "If you want to build a ship, don't drum up people to collect wood and don't assign them tasks and work, but rather teach them to long for the endless immensity of the sea." A leader must be able to clearly communicate their vision and inspire their team to work towards a common goal. Clear communication is not only important for achieving success but also for building a positive and cohesive team. As a leader, it is important to constantly strive to improve your communication skills and create an environment of open and effective communication within your team.

Overcoming the fear of failure as a leader

Overcoming the fear of failure as a leader is a critical aspect of personal and professional growth. Failure is inevitable in any endeavor, and leaders must be able to confront and overcome it in order to achieve success. Unfortunately, fear of failure is a common obstacle that holds many leaders back. It can manifest in a variety of ways, from procrastination and indecision to self-doubt and anxiety. However, by understanding and addressing the root causes of this fear, leaders can learn to overcome it and unlock their full potential.

The first step in overcoming the fear of failure as a leader is to understand the source of this fear. In many cases, it is rooted in a belief that failure is a reflection of personal inadequacy. Leaders may believe that if they fail, it means they are not good enough or not cut out for the role. However, this is a flawed and limiting belief. Failure is not a reflection of personal worth, but rather a natural and necessary part of growth and learning.

To overcome this fear, leaders must learn to reframe their perspective on failure. Instead of seeing it as a personal failure, they must view it as a valuable learning opportunity. This shift in mindset can be challenging, but it is essential for personal and professional growth. As the French author and philosopher, Andre Gide, once said, "Man cannot discover new oceans unless he has the courage to lose sight of the shore."

In addition to reframing their perspective on failure, leaders must also learn to take calculated risks. Fear of failure often stems from a fear of the unknown and an unwillingness to take risks. However, taking risks is an essential part of growth and progress. Leaders must learn to recognize when a risk is worth taking and then take action. As the French writer, Antoine de Saint-Exupéry, once said, "A goal without a plan is just a wish."

Another important aspect of overcoming the fear of failure as a leader is to develop a strong sense of self-awareness. Self-awareness allows leaders to recognize and understand their own emotions and thoughts, and to take responsibility for their actions. By becoming more self-aware, leaders can learn to recognize when they are being held back by fear and take steps to overcome it.

Furthermore, it is important for leaders to surround themselves with supportive and positive people. Having a strong support system can provide valuable guidance, encouragement, and accountability. It can also serve as a reminder that failure is not a reflection of personal worth, but rather a normal and expected part of the journey to success. As the French philosopher, Albert Camus, once said, "Don't walk behind me; I may not lead. Don't walk in front of me; I may not follow. Just walk beside me and be my friend."

In addition, leaders should also seek out mentors and role models who have successfully overcome their own fears of failure. Learning from their experiences and strategies can provide valuable insights and guidance. Furthermore, seeking guidance from experts in the field can help leaders to develop new skills, strategies and knowledge to tackle the challenges they face.

Finally, it is important for leaders to practice resilience and perseverance. Failure is not the end, it is the beginning of a new learning opportunity. Resilience and perseverance are key attributes that help leaders to get back up after falling down and to keep moving forward. This can be accomplished by setting small and achievable goals, celebrating small wins and learning from setbacks.

In conclusion, overcoming the fear of failure as a leader is a process that requires effort, commitment and a change in mindset. By understanding the source of fear, reframing perspective, taking calculated risks, developing self-awareness, surrounding oneself with supportive people, seeking guidance and mentorship, practicing resilience and perseverance, leaders can learn to overcome the fear of failure and unlock their full potential. As the French author, Victor Hugo, once said, "Nothing is more powerful than an idea whose time has come."

The power of mentorship and coaching in leadership development

Mentorship and coaching are powerful tools in the development of leaders. They provide individuals with guidance, support, and a sounding board for their ideas and decisions. Through mentorship and coaching, leaders are able to gain new perspectives, build their skills and confidence, and grow as individuals.

One of the key benefits of mentorship is the ability for leaders to gain a new perspective on their role and responsibilities. A mentor can provide guidance and advice based on their own experiences and successes, allowing the mentee to see their own challenges and opportunities from a different angle. As the French author, Antoine de Saint-Exupéry, famously said, "If you want to build a ship, don't drum up people to collect wood and don't assign them tasks and work, but rather teach them to long for the endless immensity of the sea." A mentor can help leaders to see the bigger picture and to envision new possibilities for themselves and their organizations.

Coaching, on the other hand, is more focused on helping leaders to build specific skills and to achieve specific goals. A coach can provide support, guidance, and feedback to help leaders to improve their performance and to reach their full potential. As the French author, Albert Camus, noted, "The only way to deal with an unfree world is to become so absolutely free that your very existence is an act of rebellion." A coach can help leaders to develop the skills and mindset they need to break free from limiting beliefs and to achieve true success.

Mentorship and coaching can also help leaders to build their confidence and to become more self-aware. Through the guidance and support of a mentor or coach, leaders can gain a deeper understanding of their strengths and weaknesses, and learn how to leverage their talents to become more effective leaders. The French author, Victor Hugo, once said, "He who opens a school door, closes a prison." In the same way, a mentor or coach can help leaders to open the door to new opportunities and possibilities, and to break free from the limitations that hold them back.

One practical example of the power of mentorship and coaching in leadership development is the example of the French businessman, Jean-Claude Decaux. Jean-Claude was mentored by his father, who was also a businessman. He learned from his father how to make strategic business decisions, how to build a successful company culture, and how to effectively lead and manage a team. Under his father's guidance, Jean-Claude was able to take the family business, JCDecaux, to new heights of success and to become one of the most innovative and influential leaders in the advertising and outdoor media industry.

Another practical example of the power of mentorship and coaching can be seen in the example of French soccer player, Zinedine Zidane. Zidane was mentored by several coaches throughout his career, including Arsène Wenger, who helped him to develop his skills as a midfielder and to become one of the most successful and respected players of his generation. Through the guidance and support of these coaches, Zidane was able to lead his teams to numerous victories, including the World Cup in 1998, and to become one of the greatest players in the history of French soccer.

In conclusion, mentorship and coaching play a vital role in the development of leaders. They provide individuals with guidance, support, and a sounding board for their ideas and decisions, allowing them to gain new perspectives, build their skills, and grow as individuals. As French authors such as Antoine de Saint-Exupéry, Albert Camus, Victor Hugo have noted, mentorship and coaching can help leaders to see the bigger picture, to envision new possibilities, to break free from limiting beliefs, to open new doors and to become truly effective leaders.

The role of humility in effective leadership

Humility is often overlooked as a key trait in effective leadership, yet it is one of the most essential qualities a leader can possess. Humility allows a leader to put the needs of their team and organization before their own, to admit mistakes and take responsibility for them, and to continuously seek out opportunities for growth and improvement. In this article, we will explore the role of humility in effective leadership and provide practical examples and quotes from renowned French authors to illustrate its importance.

First, let's define humility. Humility is the quality of being humble, modest, and unassuming. It is the opposite of arrogance and egotism. A humble leader recognizes their limitations and is open to learning from others. They do not see themselves as above their team or organization and are willing to take on any task, no matter how small or insignificant. This type of leader is able to build trust and respect with their team by being approachable and willing to listen.

In contrast, an arrogant leader may have a tendency to micromanage, make decisions without consulting their team, and take credit for the successes of their team without recognizing the contributions of others. This type of leader is not well-liked or respected and can create a toxic work environment.

French author and philosopher, Jean-Jacques Rousseau, wrote, "True humility is not the abject fear of being inferior, but the rational recognition of our own imperfections." This quote highlights the importance of self-awareness in humility. A humble leader is aware of their own strengths and weaknesses and is not afraid to admit them. They understand that they do not have all the answers and are willing to seek out the expertise of others.

French author and poet, Albert Camus, wrote, "The greatest wisdom is to realize one's own ignorance." This quote highlights the importance of being open-minded in humility. A humble leader is open to new ideas and perspectives and is not afraid to change their mind when presented with new information. They understand that there is always more to learn and are willing to learn from others.

One practical example of humility in leadership can be seen in the story of General George C. Marshall. During World War II, General Marshall was tasked with creating a plan to defeat Germany. Instead of relying solely on his own knowledge and expertise, he gathered a team of experts from various fields and disciplines to help him formulate the plan. He listened to their input and incorporated their suggestions into the final plan. This team-oriented approach not only led to the successful defeat of Germany, but it also demonstrated General Marshall's humility in recognizing that he couldn't do it alone and that the expertise of others was crucial in achieving success.

Another example of humility in leadership can be seen in the story of Steve Jobs, the former CEO of Apple. Jobs was known for being a demanding and demanding leader, but he also had a strong sense of humility. He was open to feedback from his team and willing to admit when he was wrong. He was also not afraid to pivot the company's direction when he realized it was not working. This humility allowed him to lead Apple to become one of the most successful companies in the world.

In conclusion, humility is a vital trait in effective leadership. A humble leader is able to build trust and respect with their team, admit mistakes and take responsibility for them, and continuously seek out opportunities for growth and improvement. French authors such as Jean-Jacques Rousseau and Albert Camus have emphasized the importance of humility in their work, and practical examples like General George C. Marshall and Steve Jobs show us how humility can lead to success in leadership.

The importance of ongoing learning and development in leadership

Learning and development is essential for any leader who wants to be successful in today's fast-paced and ever-changing business environment. The ability to adapt and evolve is crucial for staying ahead of the curve, and continuing to grow as a leader is key to achieving this.

One of the most important aspects of ongoing learning and development is the ability to stay current with the latest trends and best practices in your industry. This means that leaders must be constantly on the lookout for new information, be it through reading industry publications, attending conferences, or networking with other leaders in their field.

In addition to staying current, ongoing learning and development also involves the ability to reflect on past experiences and use them to make better decisions in the future. This means that leaders must be willing to take a critical look at their own actions and the actions of their team, and use what they learn to improve their leadership strategies.

One practical example of ongoing learning and development in leadership can be seen in the example of a CEO who, despite having years of experience in their field, realizes they are not familiar with the latest technologies. They decide to take a course to learn about the latest technologies and how they can be implemented in their company. This will not only help them stay current, but it will also give them new insights that they can apply to their leadership style and decision-making.

Another example of ongoing learning and development can be seen in the example of a manager who is struggling to lead a team that is not performing well. Instead of continuing to use the same leadership strategies that are not working, this manager decides to take a course on team management and learns new strategies for motivating and leading a team. This knowledge helps the manager to turn their team around and achieve better results.

As French author, Antoine de Saint-Exupery said, "If you want to build a ship, don't drum up people to collect wood and don't assign them tasks and work, but rather teach them to long for the endless immensity of the sea." Similarly, leadership development is not only about assigning tasks but also about teaching individuals to constantly strive for self-improvement, and leading by example.

Another renowned French author, Albert Camus, in his book "The Myth of Sisyphus," wrote, "The struggle itself toward the heights is enough to fill a man's heart. One must imagine Sisyphus happy." The same can be said for leadership development, the journey itself is what makes the leader more capable and fulfilled.

In conclusion, ongoing learning and development is essential for any leader who wants to be successful in today's fast-paced and ever-changing business environment. It is important for leaders to stay current with the latest trends and best practices in their industry and to reflect on past experiences to make better decisions in the future. By embracing ongoing learning and development, leaders can continue to grow, adapt, and evolve, which is crucial for staying ahead of the curve and achieving success.

Conclusion: Embracing Your Lone Wolf Identity and Achieving Success.

The Lone Wolf is a powerful and mysterious figure in the animal kingdom, known for its independence and self-reliance. This creature is often seen as a symbol of strength, resilience, and success, and it has been revered throughout history for its ability to survive and thrive on its own terms.

As a human being, you too possess the qualities of the Lone Wolf. You are capable of great strength and resilience, and you can achieve success in your own unique way. However, society often tries to suppress these qualities, encouraging you to conform to a certain set of norms and expectations.

In order to embrace your Lone Wolf identity and achieve success, you must first understand and accept that you are different from the pack. You are not meant to follow the same path as everyone else, and that is okay. Your path will be unique, and it will require you to think and act differently from others.

The next step is to embrace your independence and self-reliance. The Lone Wolf does not rely on anyone else for survival, and neither should you. You are the only one who can truly control your own destiny, and you must be willing to take risks and make difficult decisions in order to achieve your goals.

It is also important to remember that success is not just about achieving material wealth or status. True success is about finding and living your purpose, and doing so in a way that is authentic and true to yourself. The Lone Wolf is not concerned with fitting in or pleasing others, and neither should you.

In order to achieve success as a Lone Wolf, you must also be willing to face your fears and overcome obstacles. The Lone Wolf is not afraid to take on a challenge, and neither should you. You must be willing to push yourself out of your comfort zone and take on the difficult tasks that others are unwilling to tackle.

Finally, it is important to remember that the Lone Wolf is not alone. It has a deep connection to its pack, and it is always looking out for the well-being of its fellow wolves. As a Lone Wolf, you too must remember to connect with others and to be a positive force in the world.

In conclusion, embracing your Lone Wolf identity and achieving success is not easy, but it is possible. It requires you to be different, independent, self-reliant, and authentic. It also requires you to take risks, face your fears, and connect with others. If you are willing to do these things, you will be able to achieve success in your own unique way, and you will live a life that is true to yourself.

www.ingramcontent.com/pod-product-compliance
Lightning Source LLC
LaVergne TN
LVHW090931150826
845672LV00006B/1477

* 9 7 9 8 3 7 5 0 7 8 6 9 4 *